PEABODY JOURNAL OF EDUCATION

Camilla Benbow, Dean, Peabody College
James Guthrie, Editor
Jason Walton, Associate Editor
Rosie Moody, Coordinating Editor

SUBSCRIBER INFORMATION

Peabody Journal of Education (ISSN 0161-956X) is published quarterly by Lawrence Erlbaum Associates, Inc. (10 Industrial Avenue, Mahwah, NJ 07430-2262), and subscriptions for the 2002 volume are available on a calendar-year basis. In the United States and Canada, per-volume rates are U.S. $50 for individuals, U.S. $25 for graduate students, and U.S. $245 for institutions; in other countries, per-volume rates are U.S. $80 for individuals, U.S. $50 for graduate students, and U.S. $275 for institutions. Send subscription orders, information requests, and address changes to the Journal Subscription Department, Lawrence Erlbaum Associates, Inc., 10 Industrial Avenue, Mahwah, NJ 07430-2262. Address changes should include the mailing label or a facsimile. Claims for missing issues cannot be honored beyond 4 months after mailing date. Duplicate copies cannot be sent to replace issues not delivered due to failure to notify publisher of change of address.

Electronic: Full-price print subscribers to Volume 77, 2002 are entitled to receive the electronic version free of charge. *Electronic-only* subscriptions are also available at a reduced price of $220.50 for institutions and $45 for individuals. *Peabody Journal of Education* is abstracted or indexed in: *Linguistics and Language Behavior Abstracts; Contents Pages in Education; Sociological Abstracts; Education Index; Education Abstracts; Social Services Abstracts.* Microform copies of this journal are available through ProQuest Information and Learning, P.O. Box 1346, Ann Arbor, MI 48106-1346. For more information, call 1-800-521-0600 x2888.

Copyright © 2002, Lawrence Erlbaum Associates, Inc. No part of this publication may be reproduced, in any form or by any means, without permission of the publisher.

Send special requests for permission to the Permissions Department, Lawrence Erlbaum Associates, Inc., 10 Industrial Avenue, Mahwah, NJ 07430-2262.

Journal Project Supervisor: Mary A. Araneo, Lawrence Erlbaum Associates, Inc.

PEABODY JOURNAL OF EDUCATION

Volume 77, Number 1, 2002

Leadership Challenges in Creating Inclusive School Environments

Introduction: Leadership and Diversity:
Creating Inclusive Schools   1
Jean A. Madsen
Reitumetse Obakeng Mabokela

Teachers' Perceptions of African American Principals'
Leadership in Urban Schools   7
Cornel Jones

African American Leaders' Perceptions of Intergroup
Conflict   35
Jean A. Madsen
Reitumetse Obakeng Mabokela

Teachers' Perceptions of Intergroup Conflict in Urban
Schools   59
Stella C. Bell

Urban School Leaders and the Implementation of Zero-
Tolerance Policies: An Examination of Its Implications   82
Christopher Dunbar, Jr.
Francisco A. Villarruel

Introduction: Leadership and Diversity: Creating Inclusive Schools

Jean A. Madsen
Texas A & M University

Reitumetse Obakeng Mabokela
Michigan State University

Increasing diversity among teachers and students is one of the most critical adaptive challenges that schools face. Ethnic differences between teachers and school leaders may result in either expectations or working styles that may influence their response to students of color. As educators, it is important to understand the meaning and implications of teaching

---

The coeditors and the contributors would like to acknowledge various people who played an important role in putting together this special issue. First, we would like to thank Jennifer Barratt for her endless energy in editing multiple revisions. She was a wonderful organizer and kept us centered. Another person is Bill Ashworth, who willingly took on this project in addition to his other duties. He spent considerable time reading and rereading work and provided constructive feedback. We also would like to thank members of the Urban Advisory Group, who we asked to read articles and give us their feedback. In addition, we would like to thank Rosie Moody, Jason Walton, and James Guthrie for their support in asking us to put together this special issue. They were helpful in getting us information and provided a supportive environment for our work. Finally, we also would all like to thank our family members and friends, who put up with our long hours, provided support, and listened endlessly to our concerns.

Requests for reprints should be sent to Jean A. Madsen, Educational Administration and Human Resource Development 4226 TAMU Texas A & M University, College Station, TX 77843.

ethnically diverse students in response to their learning needs. Thus, what is the role of school administrators in leading teachers of color and European American teachers to work collectively to meet the needs of their diverse school population?

The articles in this special issue, entitled *Leadership Challenges in Creating Inclusive School Environments,* explore the perceptions of teachers toward African American school leaders as they seek to create inclusive school environments, the capacity of teachers and school leaders to negotiate intergroup conflict so they can work collaboratively on matters of race, and leaders' interpretation and implementation of policies that influence the educational experiences and outcomes of students of color. These new directions for leadership require school administrators to foster new meanings about diversity; to establish an inclusive culture; and to consider issues related to democracy, social justice, and teaching and learning (Riehl, 2000; Shields, 2000).

Leadership and diversity are invariably connected as schools move from monocultural, nondiverse contexts to those that contain ethnically diverse, multilingual, and economically disadvantaged children. Therefore, as we prepare leaders, there needs to be a commitment to valuing diversity by providing training to school leaders to respond to diversity challenges. One can argue that in leading a diverse group of teachers and students, leaders must be knowledgeable about school participants' ethnic and cultural differences to ensure an inclusive school. Therefore, a new leadership framework should focus on the impact of diversity dimensions that involve strategic, structural, cultural, and personnel considerations in managing schools.

Diversity perspectives pose challenges to many traditional beliefs in organization and management. Researchers have noted that diversity initiatives such as valuing diversity may have implications for how managers lead their organizations on these concerns. Consequently, diversity perspectives may challenge present mainstream leadership theories as they recognize structural and cultural dimensions (Chen & Van Velsor, 1996). Thus, one can argue that developing skills of organizing and managing diverse employees fall in the domain of leadership.

The intersection of mainstream leadership theories and diversity research implies contrasting perspectives. Mainstream leadership theories and research perceive leadership at interpersonal and intrapersonal levels but rarely as an intergroup focus. Therefore, mainstream theories define leadership in terms of personality characteristics and how leaders use those abilities to influence their relationship with their employees. Mainstream theories do not look beyond the leader–follower relationship and the impact that it has on organizational identities. Mainstream leadership theories focus on the rational, purposeful, and goal-oriented leadership processes (Chemers & Murphy, 1995).

In contrast, diversity research examines how social, racial, and cultural issues that originate outside the organizational boundaries affect leader–member interactions. Diversity research has found effects of race and gender on organizational networks, career opportunities, mentoring relations, employee perceptions, values, and communication styles (Chemers, Oskamp, & Constanzo, 1995; Chen & Van Velsor, 1996; Cox, 1994). Therefore, leaders who work with members of different ethnic backgrounds need to recognize cultural differences in their followers that may affect the ways in which relationships are developed and negotiated. Consequently, we need to recognize the importance of social group identity in leading diverse groups within the organization.

Unlike mainstream leadership theories, diversity research emphasizes group identities and views them as cultural identities. The concept of cultural identity can serve as a psychological lens to examine the experience and impact of diversity at the level of the individual while maintaining in focus the reality of group-level differences (Ferdman, 1995). The intercultural view emphasizes that we are all cultural beings, shaped and oriented by the cultures of the groups to which we belong (Ferdman, 1995). By understanding cultural differences among groups, there are implications for interpersonal and organizational processes and outcomes when members of these groups work together or come in contact with each other. This approach implies looking at individuals in the context of their particular groups and being cognizant and sensitive to their group membership (Ferdman, 1995).

Embedded intergroup relations theory further delineates organizational groups from identity groups. Like cultural identities, identity groups share common biological characteristics such as gender, ethnicity, and age; have similar historical experiences; and are subjected to similar social forces (Alderfer, 1987). An organizational group is one in which members share common organizational positions and participate in equivalent work experiences. People's identities in organizations are a function of their organization group membership (Nkomo & Cox, 1996). The identity of an individual in the organization is determined not only by organizational categorization but also identity group membership.

Educational organizations that reflect diversity of class, gender, socioeconomic status, and nationality establish a complex set of interactions that have implications for how groups are formed. Intergroup theory applies to school participants because of the nature of the organizational context between identity and organizational groups. In schools, a teaching culture exists that imposes beliefs about appropriate ways of educating children and results in norms of actions. Critical to this dimension are the personal and professional experiences of most teachers that focus on European American students with little attention to students of color. According to Lewis (2001), the fostering and enabling of a "color-blind" ideology allows most teachers to see themselves as racially neutral and deserving of their own success and not responsible for the exclusion of others. Due to this view, schools maintain a strong organizational culture that is developed and maintained through the selection and retention process (Schneider, 1987) that seeks to reinforce the existing school culture.

Overview of Articles

Chemers (1993) outlined three pervasive leadership functions that he believes are important for a person to lead an ethnically diverse workforce. Ethnic differences between leaders and followers may result in leadership expectations or working interactions that may affect high-quality exchanges (Linden, Wayne, & Stillwell, 1993). In the first article, "Teachers' Perceptions of African American Principals' Leadership in Urban Schools," Jones examines the complex dynamics of how diverse followers perceive their African American principals. Findings from this study revealed some of the challenges that African American principals undergo in their daily efforts to create inclusive school environments. In leading a diverse workforce, both leaders of color and their European American counterparts need to understand the complexities of leading a diverse group of followers. As this study revealed, the leaders' ethnicity had an impact on how they interacted with and were perceived by their followers. Therefore, in leading a diverse workforce, school administrators need to be sensitive to workplace differences and must be able to reduce negative stereotypes. Leadership in diverse organizations includes the orientations and behaviors appropriate to establish open and authentic relationships among a diverse group of school participants.

Intergroup theory helps us understand the effects of diverse identities in the workplace. When people of different ethnic groups interact with each other, there is an increased potential for intergroup conflict (Ayman, 1993). Intergroup theory, leadership, and diversity are invariably connected. So the question arises, do school leaders and teachers perceive intergroup conflict differently? Madsen and Mabokela's article, "African American Leaders' Perceptions of Intergroup Conflict," revealed multiple sources of intergroup conflict that influenced their leadership decisions. In this study, these leaders experienced incompatible goals between themselves and their school participants, which resulted in group boundaries and cultural differences. These leaders struggled with power differences with their majority school population and its impact on their ability to effectively facilitate intercultural contact among identity and organizational groups.

In the third article, "Teachers' Perceptions of Intergroup Conflict in Urban Schools," Bell examines how teachers of color and European American teachers perceive intergroup conflict among and between their groups. The study revealed multiple sources of intergroup conflict that resulted, at times, in a negative relationship between these groups of teachers. These teachers identified similar experiences in how they perceived intergroup conflict but expressed them differently. Their differences centered on how they perceived their own interests relative to how they worked with students of color. Group boundaries were developed when the teachers of color noted their roles as cultural translators and the importance of their ethnic identity in interacting with students. Consequently, European American teachers' color-blind approach often created intergroup conflict among these groups of teachers.

The final article, "Urban School Leaders and the Implementation of Zero-Tolerance Policies: An Examination of Its Implications," examines how administrators in an urban school context interpret and subsequently implement the zero-tolerance policy. Dunbar and Villarruel highlight the critical role of principals in the implementation of this policy and its ultimate impact on the educational experiences of students of color. Findings from this study revealed that principals often used incongruent interpretations, resulting in its inequitable application. Other factors, such as the student's age, grade level, social background, and the lack of awareness (among principals) about the serious implications of this policy, influenced the principals' decisions on how to enforce it. In essence, the findings reveal that the disparate interpretation of this policy negatively influences the educational experience of students of color in urban schools.

Summary

As coeditors, our primary objective has been to share a series of research articles that address the complexity of diversity and leadership in providing inclusive and responsive school environments for all children. These articles highlight critical concerns that confront leaders as they seek to create inclusive school cultures. They specifically reveal the complex dynamics that must be negotiated as leaders seek to respond to the divergent needs of their various constituents. As schools seek solutions to respond to students, leaders need to embrace communities of difference where both minority and majority groups can be nurtured and flourish. Given the complexity of these articles, we hope readers will reflect on these readings and be willing to envision a new direction in how leaders will address race in creating inclusive schools.

References

Alderfer, C. P. (1987). An intergroup perspective on group dynamics. In J. Lorsch (Ed.), *Handbook of organizational behavior* (pp. 190–222). Englewood Cliffs, NJ: Prentice Hall.

Ayman, R. (1993). Leadership perceptions: The role of gender and culture. In M. Chemers & R. Ayman (Eds.), *Leadership theory and research: Perspectives and directions* (pp. 137–166). San Diego, CA: Academic.

Chemers, M. (1993). An integrative theory of leadership. In M. Chemers & R. Ayman (Eds.), *Leadership theory and research: Perspectives and directions* (pp. 239–319). San Diego, CA: Academic.

Chemers, M. M., & Murphy, S. E. (1995). Leadership and diversity in groups and organizations. In M. M. Chemers, S. Oskamp, & M. A. Constanzo (Eds.), *Diversity in organizations: New perspectives for a changing workplace* (pp. 157–190). Thousand Oaks, CA: Sage.

Chemers, M., Oskamp, S. G., & Constanzo, M. (1995). *Diversity in organizations: New perspectives for a changing workplace*. Thousand Oaks, CA: Sage.

Chen, C., & Van Velsor, E. (1996). New directions for research and practice in diversity leadership. *Leadership Quarterly, 7*, 285–302.

Cox, T. (1994). *Cultural diversity in organizations: Theory, research, and practice*. San Francisco: Berrett-Koehler.

Ferdman, B. M. (1995). Cultural identity and diversity in organizations: Bridging the gap between group differences and individual uniqueness. In M. M. Chemers, S. Oskamp, & M. A. Constanzo (Eds.), *Diversity in organizations: New perspectives for a changing workplace* (pp. 37–61). Thousand Oaks, CA: Sage.

Lewis, A. (2001). There is no "race" in the schoolyard: Color-blind ideology in an (almost) all-white school. *American Educational Research Association, 38*, 781–811.

Linden, R. C., Wayne, S. J., & Stillwell, D. (1993). A longitudinal study on the early development of leader member exchanges. *Journal of Applied Psychology, 78*, 662–674.

Nkomo, S., & Cox, T. (1996). Diverse identities in organizations. In S. Clegg, C. Hardy, & W. Nords (Eds.), *Handbook of organization studies* (pp. 338–356). Thousand Oaks, CA: Sage.

Riehl, C. J. (2000). The principal's role in creating inclusive schools for diverse students: A review of normative, empirical, and critical literature on the practice of educational administration. *Review of Educational Research, 70*(1), 55–88.

Schneider, B. (1987). The people make the place. *Personnel Psychology, 40*, 437–453.

Shields, C. M. (2000, November). *Leadership imperatives for communities of difference*. Paper presented at the meeting of the American Educational Research Association, Albuquerque, NM.

Teachers' Perceptions of African American Principals' Leadership in Urban Schools

Cornel Jones
Texas A & M University

Concerns about leading ethnically diverse urban schools imply that principals of color may play an important role in accomplishing their schools' goals. Findings from this study revealed that in areas of image management and relationship development, teachers of color and European American teachers in urban schools perceive their principals' leadership differently. Results revealed that (a) leaders of color were critical in creating an inclusive school among groups of ethnically diverse groups of teachers; (b) due to their racial affiliation, leaders of color played an important role in recruiting and retaining teachers of color; and (c) leaders of color were responsible for ensuring that European American teachers were culturally responsive to students of color.

Our schools are undergoing monumental challenges as they evolve from monocultural nondiverse contexts to ones that contain ethnically diverse, multilingual, and economically poorer children. In leading urban schools, leaders of color must possess administrative skills to mobilize a diverse teaching staff so children in urban schools will succeed academically. Thus, if leaders of color are to play this important role, what critical functions of effective leadership are needed to work with a diverse group

---

Requests for reprints should be sent to Cornel Jones, 4001 Tanne Hill Lane, Austin, TX 78721.

of followers? The intent of this qualitative study was to examine the perceptions that teachers of color and European American teachers have about their African American principals' ability to lead successful urban schools.

The Complexity of Defining and Validating African American Principals' Leadership

African American leaders were perceived as followers under the tutelage of European American principals, and for decades their talents were measured as subpar (Foster, 1995). This inferior perception of leaders of color was prevalent in school systems throughout the United States. These exclusionary practices created an African American educational leadership vacuum throughout the country until the start of the Civil Rights movement. Rooted in the dual school systems of the past, European American colleagues considered African American principals as insignificant in leadership roles (Delpit, 1995). Sizemore (1986) also found that African Americans were perceived by their counterparts as "lesser leaders" in the world of school leadership.

Counter to these beliefs about leaders of color, Lomotey (1989) discovered differences in leadership approaches between leaders of color and European American principals. He noted that African American principals have a strong commitment to African American students and a deep understanding that these students can learn. Lomotey also noted that African American principals placed a higher priority on community involvement than their European American peers. Valverde (1987) discovered that African American principals functioned as role models who encouraged positive teacher–student relationships in the classroom. Additionally, Pollard (1997) noted that an African American principal's ethnic identity shaped the social constructs of his or her administrative role and defined his or her mission for schools. As a result, life experiences have a major impact on a person's leadership orientation (Lomotey, 1989).

Unable to explain the success of leaders of color despite barriers and social constructs through traditional leadership characteristics models, researchers sought alternative approaches. Banks (1991) found the traditional approaches to leadership, such as power-influence, traits or characteristics, behavioral, or situational (contingency) models rely too heavily on the individual perspectives of the Eurocentric view of leadership. Many of these models focused on the leader as the key to the success of the organization. However, the new approach based its explanation not on the leaders' individual leadership characteristics, but first on the comparative perspective of community. In short, leaders of color look to the community to assist in their efforts to change the academic and social climate of the school. From this new approach, a second notion regarding success by leaders of color was developed.

The notion that principals have different roles based on their ethnic background and experiences gained in popularity (Bass, 1985; Conger & Kanungo, 1988). From the literature, scholars found that a person's socialization has an impact on the perception of and interaction with people who are ethnically, culturally, and socially different. Therefore, as people are socialized about others dissimilar to themselves, they make value judgments, character assessments, and stereotypical comments (Banks, 1991). Banks (1991) contended that this socialization about others leads them to make cultural assumptions, especially about people of color. These global labels manifest themselves in how people treat and respond to each other in the organization.

Finally, concerns about leading diverse organizations imply that leaders of color may play an important role in accomplishing the organization's goals (Cox, 1994). However, due to stereotypes about leaders of color that followers may have about them, these leaders' credibility may be damaged. Sizemore (1986) found that leaders of color face loyalty issues (i.e., leadership image, bureaucratic ideologies) in the organization that clash with their own socialized beliefs (ethnic kinship, culture). Therefore, as our ethnically socialized constructs of African American leaders change, so must our perceptions about their leadership.

Chemers's Integrative Leadership Model

As a way to frame African American principals' leadership in urban schools, Chemers's model of integrative leadership was used. Chemers (1993) outlined three pervasive leadership functions that he believes are necessary for a person to lead an ethnically diverse workforce. The first category, image management, reminds us that leadership is a process of social influence whereby leaders induce followers to apply their energies and resources toward a collective objective (Chemers & Murphy, 1995). Therefore, the perceptions of the leader by his or her followers indicate the basis to evaluate his or her credibility. Also, perceptions by followers are often affected by differences in assumptions and expectations about leadership. Thus, leaders in diverse organizations need to be seen as credible, having the expertise to accomplish the group's goals and mission, and trustable.

Relationship development is the second category of the integrative model. It focuses on the quality of the relationship between leader and followers and assesses how the leader motivates followers, evaluates their performances, and creates a high comfort level among all in the organization. As a result, the relationship's quality level often determines the followers' commitment to achieve the organization's goals (Chemers & Murphy, 1995). In diverse organizations, relationship development may be affected by the followers' reactions to the leader's behavior, the leader's ability to assess their followers' needs, and the followers' feelings that their needs have or have not been met. Ethnic differences between leader and followers may result in leadership expectations or working interactions that may affect high-quality exchanges (Linden, Wayne, & Stillwell, 1993). Additionally, these feelings usually surface during times of conflict when followers perceive that they are treated unfairly, during downturns in the economy, or during cultural misunderstandings.

The third category, team coordination and deployment, describes the leader's ability to use his or her talents and resources of followers to accomplish organizational objectives (Chemers & Murphy, 1995). Therefore, the focus is on accomplishing organizational goals through the collective performances of diverse people within the organization. In this vein, leaders of color face challenges to their role in diverse contexts. The quality of leadership between leaders and followers becomes complicated when conflicts arise between ethnically diverse groups in the organization.

To understand how diverse followers perceive African American principals in urban schools, Chemers's (1993) integrative leadership model was used to analyze the data. Chemers's leadership model provides a framework through which African American principals' leadership was examined. In leading a diverse workforce, leaders need to be sensitive to workplace differences among followers and must be able to reduce negative stereotypes as well. Leadership in diverse organizations includes the orientations and behaviors appropriate to establish open and authentic relationships among diverse groups of followers. Thus, for leaders to be effective in diverse organizations, they must develop an empowerment model that enables and motivates followers by increasing their personal efficacy.

Methodology

Data Collection

This qualitative study used multiple sources for its data collection methods. For this research, a case study is defined as a single entity, a unit of similar participants within the bounded context of urban schools (Merriam, 1988). This was a comprehensive study that examined teachers' perceptions of their principals' leadership and how their principals responded to their teachers' responses. Data collection methods for this overall study included the use of questionnaires, personal interviews, observations, reflective journals, and written artifacts. Information was collected over the course of 4 months during the 2000–2001 school year.

Data discussed in this study were part of a larger study. However, this study draws on the teachers' interviews and their perceptions about their African American principals' leadership in urban schools. Early in this study a questionnaire was developed to introduce the participants to the topic and to determine their preliminary impressions about their African American principals' leadership. After the questionnaires were reviewed, interview questions were developed to respond to these teachers' perceptions. Also, the interview questions were developed based on Chemers's (1993) three categories of image management, relationship development, and team coordination.

The initial interview was designed to elicit from each teacher a description of his or her perceptions about their African American principals' leadership. The second interview gave the researcher the opportunity to clarify teachers' perceptions and to address their interactions with their principals. During the final interview, participants were asked to share their feelings about their perceptions as compared to their ethnically diverse colleagues. Initial and final interviews lasted approximately 1 hr. Most interviews were taped and later transcribed for analysis.

During the data collection phase, several teachers' interviews took a somewhat "out of the normal" interview procedure. A possible explanation may include that several of the European American teachers felt uncomfortable discussing their perceptions of an African American with the African American researcher. During these nine interviews, the researcher had to conduct them without audiotaping or writing devices. The breakdown of alternative data collection methods were as follows: (a) Four follow-up interviews were conducted over the telephone because the teachers did not want to be interviewed face to face. Each participant was asked the same questions. (b) Three teachers prohibited the researchers from taking notes during their interviews. After these participants' interviews were conducted, field notes were made. (c) With the final interview, two teachers requested that they would only respond to follow-up questions in written form.

Data Sources

Schools' and principals' profiles. The initial phase of the research consisted of identifying successful urban schools administered by African American principals in a southern urban school district. The criteria used to identify the urban schools were as follows: (a) headed by an African American principal with 3 or more years of administrative experience; (b) contained an ethnically diverse staff of both teachers of color and European American teachers; (c) considered as having an acceptable or higher academic rating during the past 2 years per the state's accountability system; and (d) consisted of an ethnically diverse student population. Based on these established criteria, nine schools were identified, but only seven schools agreed to participate in this research.

The seven urban schools that participated in this project were similar in their demographic representation. Originally, six of the seven had histories of high student and teacher mobility, low academic achievement, little parental involvement, a large percentage of economically disadvantaged minority students, and poor instructional facilities. Although the seventh school identified for this project had been in existence for only 3 years, this school had similar histories as the other schools. Within the first 2 years under these seven African American principals' leadership, their students' academic achievement increased as measured by the state's criteria tests, staff and student mobility decreased, and each school received an acceptable or higher rating on the state's accountability report.

The seven African American principals had 5 years or more of administrative experience in leading diverse schools. The average number of years of leadership in these schools was 7. There were one male and six female principals ranging from 7 to 24 years of administrative experience. All of the schools were located in depressed areas of the district. Also, most of the facilities were in need of renovation.

Teacher participants' selection. Initially, the researcher solicited the principals' advice for selecting teacher participants. This was to ensure that teacher participants would reflect a cross-section of gender, ethnicity, diversity of leadership roles, and years of experience to speak about their principals' leadership. Based on the initial teacher candidate list, the researcher identified only those candidates that he felt could provide insights on their leadership ability. Although more than 70 teachers were identified based on the selection criteria, only 30 were chosen to participate in this study. Of the 30 teachers, only those who were viewed as teacher leaders, represented the school's staff diversity, and had approximately 2 or more years of teaching experience were identified. Overall, of the 30 teachers, there were a total of 15 male and female European American teachers and 15 male and female African American teachers.

European American teachers. Two European American male and 13 female teachers were interviewed for this study. All of the European American teachers had 2 or more years of teaching experience. One of the European American men taught at the elementary level for approximately 4 years, whereas the other male participant taught at the middle school for over 10 years. Both of the European American men were educated outside the district. One of the European American men relocated from the Northeast, and the other male participant was from a small town in this state. Neither of the 2 male European American participants had worked in diverse situations until they had taken their present positions.

The 13 female European American teachers were from a variety of backgrounds. Four of the European American women had previously taught in predominantly majority schools during their careers, and the other 9 had taught in schools with diverse student populations or all students of color. Most of the European American female teachers were born and educated in the state and had taught in their present schools for at least the past 2 years. Also, 4 of the female participants had relocated to this district as a result of their husbands' employment in the area.

African American teachers. Fifteen African American teachers participated in this study. There were 2 men and 13 women. All of these African American participants had 2 or more years of teaching experience. Both of the African American men taught at the elementary level for less than 4 years. One of the male African American teachers was a retired military officer from the Midwest. The other African American male teacher had worked in the private sector for 15 years and was from a small town in the state where this study took place.

The 13 female African American teachers varied in backgrounds much like their European American counterparts. Seven had taught for more than 20 years in urban areas. Three of the African American teachers had graduated from historically black colleges. Three of the African American respondents had taught in segregated situations prior to districtwide integration in the 1970s. One African American teacher grew up in a predominantly European American community and attended only affluent, suburban schools. About half of the African American women were born and educated in the state where this study took place, whereas the other half were from other states. All of the African American women chose to teach at their present school.

Data Analysis

A qualitative thematic strategy of data analysis was used to categorize and make judgments about the interpretation of the data. This methodological process led to a single-case level of analysis where data were aggregated to incorporate a thematic approach. This analytical procedure allowed important themes and categories to emerge inductively from the data across cases. The findings from the interviews were clustered by key themes across schools and single cases. The researchers used the prior-research driven approach to identify themes and to develop a coding process (Boyatzis, 1998). In establishing the reliability for this study, the data were analyzed using what Conrad (1982) called a constant comparative method. This coding process was constructed by comparing the teachers' perceptions about their principals' leadership with Chemers's (1993) integrative model. By building on Chemers's work, this provides a framework to examine how African American principals in urban schools are perceived in their ability to lead both teachers of color and European American teachers (Table 1).

The conceptually organized themes were clustered around related characteristics and the identification of an underlying construct (Boyatzis, 1998). An analysis of the participants' responses was based on transcribed taped interviews, field notes, and document analysis. Data analysis of the findings closely followed themes that evolved from Chemers's (1993) model. The interview questions were indexed against each participant's

Table 1

Chemers's (1993) Integrative Leadership Model: Image Management, Relationship Development, and Team Coordination and Deployment

Theme	Leadership Features	Areas Analyzed
Image management	Communicates his or her influence with followers in the organization	Legitimacy Trustworthiness Credibility
Relationship development	Motivates followers to pursue and accomplish organizational tasks	Motivation efforts Fair evaluation Comfort level Validation/Praise
Team coordination and deployment	Coordinates group resources to achieve organizational goals	Group processes Situational control Task development

responses in narrative form to show patterns of the perceptions under the three categories (image management, relationship development, and team collaboration) about the principals' leadership. Initial themes were examined and used to construct follow-up questions for subsequent interviews of all participants. These emerged themes and copies of participants' interview transcripts were given to them for their reactions and corrections. Outlines were constructed to compare the participants' responses with the interview questions as a way to create a descriptive taxonomy. Secondary interviews with all participants were conducted to clarify emerging themes and patterns analyzed from all data sources. This process allowed the researcher to determine the degree of emerged theme validity between teachers of color and European American teachers' perceptions about their principals' leadership.

As Triandis (1993) discovered, the intent of trying to examine cultural differences is very difficult and one on which few researchers reflect. Thus, this researcher felt it was important to address cross-cultural issues in this study. The researcher is an African American man, who not only interviewed teachers of color but also European American teachers. Cross-cultural interpretations of data must be sensitive to issues of race, as this may prohibit an appropriate interpretation of the findings. The researcher addressed the cross-cultural phenomena in this study as follows: (a) teacher participants were required to disclose their ethnic identification on the questionnaire; (b) additional columns were created to reflect differences in perceptions between the two ethnic groups through the sifting and resifting process; and (c) inquiries about ethnic differences were analyzed and follow-up interviews were conducted. Once the data were examined, the researcher addressed different interpretations to validate his cross-cultural interpretation of data and to ensure a reliable and trustworthy interpretation of the findings (Merriam, 1988).

This study was conceived as an exploratory study to investigate how teachers of color and European American teachers perceive their principals' leadership in successful urban schools. For this study, the following limitations applied. The theoretical model used to analyze the collected data about the perceptions of African American principals' leadership was based on the research to examine how majority leaders manage a diverse workforce. However, for this study, this was the first time that Chemers's (1993) model was used to analyze how leaders of color are perceived in diverse organizations. Also, another limitation with this study might be that the principals originally selected the teachers for the researcher. Although the principals initially selected teachers, the researcher developed additional criteria such as types of leadership roles and willingness to share their opinions in selecting the participants. These criteria allowed the researcher to further determine how these teachers perceived their principals' leadership. As a result, a fair representation of participants from each ethnic group was chosen to share their perceptions in this study.

Findings

Based on Chemers's (1993) leadership model of how to lead a diverse workforce, this study examined how teachers of color and European American teachers perceived their African American principals' leadership. Although Chemers's model identified three categories for data analysis, only the first two are being reported in this article. The researcher felt that data collected under the last category needed additional clarification and analysis, so it was not included in this article. From the findings, the data indicated that teachers of color perceived their African American principals' leadership capacity differently than that of their European American counterparts (Table 2). These differences were in the areas of image management and relationship development.

In the area of image management, teachers of color perceived that their principals' leadership capacity was a result of their obtained position in the organization. However, the European American teachers perceived their leaders as having identifiable leadership characteristics. Data collected about the principals' relationship development revealed that teachers of color believed that they had both a positive professional and personal relationship with the African American administrators. However, differences between these two groups of participants arose in their level of professional and personal trust and validation of efforts (Table 2 summarizes the general differences of both ethnic groups).

Image Management

Chemers's (1993) model of effective leadership in the area of image management implies that the leader must establish credibility by projecting an image that followers perceive as competent, trustworthy, and believable. This leadership skill focuses on leaders' ability to deal with their followers' perceptions about them. Findings from this study revealed that both the European American and African American teachers' responses to image management were based on the following subthemes: (a) personal expectations and legitimacy of the leader, (b) level of trust between leader and followers, and (c) credibility with followers (see Table 2).

Table 2

Chemers's (1993) Integrative Leadership Model

Theme	Leadership Features	Areas Analyzed	Teachers of Color	European American Teachers
Image management	Communicates his or her influence with followers in the organization	Legitimacy	Positional in organization	Leadership characteristics
		Trustworthiness	Statue of leader	Limited trust based on situation
		Credibility	Kinship	Accomplishments and credentials
Relationship development	Motivates followers to pursue and accomplish organizational tasks	Motivation efforts	Creation of risk-taking climate	Proving themselves
		Fair evaluations	Fair evaluations	Fair after proving themselves
		Comfort level	Kinship comfort	Somewhat uncomfortable
		Validation	Little needed	Praise with efforts and experience

Leader's legitimacy. Chemers and Murphy (1995) described a leader's legitimacy in an organization as a crucial element to "social influence" over followers. The followers' perceptions of the leader had an impact on the leader's credibility and ability to lead. This subtheme revealed that teachers of color believed their principals were legitimate leaders because of their ability to accomplish tasks and due to the strong racial affiliation they had with their principal. In contrast, European American teachers' perceptions about their African American principals' legitimacy took a slightly different perspective. Findings revealed that although both novice and veteran European American teachers believed that their principals were legitimate leaders, there was no consensus among them on what that meant. Although the European American teachers as a group felt that their principals were legitimate leaders, this legitimacy was based on their socialized view (quantifiable, observable leadership characteristics, i.e., degreed, virtuous, and resolute) of the person in the position.

Teachers of color perceived their African American principals as legitimate leaders. The teachers of color gave unconditional respect to their principals. These perceptions were derived from the reverence that people of color have been socialized to believe about their leaders in any organization. This reverence is biblical in origin and manifested itself into the cultural practices of people of color. Teachers of color believed that their principals were legitimate not only through their ability to lead the school, but also because these principals were accepted by their community. In other words, teachers of color believed that their African American principals' vision was to develop both the academic and social climate of the entire community. Thus, manifestations of their leadership efforts would include empowered people through self-determination and self-worth. One teacher of color summarized her principal's legitimacy as follows:

> I think because of her respect for us . . . she treats us as adults. She treats us as individuals with the same level education. I think that you want to rise to the occasion, because she exhibits nothing but positive things in regards to us. And again, you know, when negativity arises, she does not have a fear to come to us or we go to her and say, "Okay. This is how I see this." And it's resolved. Or, she'll ask, "Are you all right with this?" And then before you leave that so-called round table, you know, you've talked about it and you do feel better. As so as a result of that, I think that you just have positive feelings about her leadership.

Furthermore, teachers of color believed that because they were of the same ethnic background as their principals, this allowed them to be more effective in their interactions with their principals. Thus, they felt that their African American principals were legitimated just on the basis of their racial affiliation. Teachers of color believed that being led by an African American principal afforded them more access to organizational information and available resources. Additionally, they felt that they could empathize with their principals' frustrations and conflicts and be used as sounding boards. As a result, they believed that due to their racial affiliation, their leaders of color would receive an understanding "ear" from them. One veteran African American teacher encapsulated her ethnic kinship view.

> We come from the same backgrounds. I know when she is down about something. It is just the way we are as African Americans. As a result, my job is to help her overcome challenges to her authority and assist her in making this school a better place to work.

In contrast, European Americans felt that the legitimacy of leaders of color was based on quantifiable leadership characteristics. However, these European American teachers were unable to agree on what these leadership abilities should be to be perceived as legitimate. Some European American teachers believed that their principals should be intelligent, strong-willed, and patient. They felt that these qualities would allow their principals to intellectually engage the staff and be steadfast in their efforts to accomplish organizational tasks. They stated that if a principal possessed these qualities, then his or her leadership would be legitimated and he or she would be able to influence followers' actions. As one veteran European American teacher described,

> I feel she's a lot like me in some way. She's very educated. She's very professional. I like all of that. I get along very well with her. Every teacher here had to show that she can do her job. So, I trust her to do the right thing for me, now and in the future. Others will have to make up their own minds about her credibility.

Other European American teachers felt that their principals' legitimacy should be based on being principled, engaged, and outgoing. Because European American teachers valued leaders who demonstrated positive personal interactions and virtues, they looked to their African American leaders as those who maintained a high moral climate. Also, these teachers believed that if they had a prolonged engagement with their leaders, they would benefit from this relationship. Although they did not have the racial affiliation with their principals, these teachers did believe that over time they were more receptive to their principals. One European American teacher voiced her perceptions as follows:

> She [the principal] always stands up for the right thing at this school. If you are wrong, she is not afraid to tell you. Many of us like her way to standing against those who try to divide us. Also, she works with anyone whether she wants to work with her or not.

Leader's trustworthiness. Another aspect of image management is the leader's trustworthiness. This is characterized by a leader's abilities to elicit followers' organizational loyalty via his or her own personal performance (Hollander, 1964). There were differences between how teachers of color and European American teachers perceived their principals as trustworthy. Due to the ethnic kinship and strong sense of racial affiliation, African American teachers developed an unconditional trust of their principals. Because there was not a racial connection, the European American teachers were hesitant to trust their principals. The data revealed that possible causal factors were fear of retaliation from their principals or being unable to meet expectations established for students of color. Nevertheless, after a period of time, European American teachers did come to have faith in how their African American principals administered the school. Although the European American teachers learned to trust their principals over time, this became problematic when principals promoted culturally relevant responses to students of color. European American teachers were uncomfortable addressing issues of race and its connection to culturally relevant instruction that may have influenced how they trusted their African American principals.

In this study, African American teachers perceived their principals as trustworthy (i.e., kept promises, mostly objectives in actions) because they kept their word and were able to accomplish their schools' goals. Teachers of color believed their principals' trustworthiness lay in their ability to accomplish organizational tasks (i.e., organized resources, mobilized staff for action). As a result, the teachers of color perceived their principals' "word" as honorable and believable based not only on their racial affiliation, but also on their ability to achieve stated goals. Furthermore, the teachers of color perceived that their principals were fair in how they allocated resources. They believed that their African American principals based their decisions on student needs, not political reasons or expedience. As a result, teachers of color felt empowered to accept challenging assignments based on their principals' previous support and role-modeling behaviors. As this teacher noted,

> She models by example. She lays out the problem, gives us challenges to overcome, and supports us in achieving them. She makes it safe for us to take instructional risks with responsibility ... A good leader lets others lead.

Another aspect of their principals' trustworthiness by teachers of color was the notion of unconditional trust and a racial affiliation. This trust, as Banks (1991) concluded, was derived from the "ethnic kinship" bonds between leader and followers of the same racial affiliation. As mentioned earlier, most people of color have been socialized to believe in the hierarchical form of leadership (Pollard, 1997). All of the teachers of color expressed unconditional trust in their principals' leadership in part due to this ethnic kinship. Also, these African American teachers viewed their principals as a "mother/father" figure in the organization. This strong sense of racial affiliation and sense of kinship implied for these teachers that their principals would take care of them in crisis and noncrisis school situations and share advice. One veteran teacher of color voiced her perception as follows:

> When I was accused of hurting a child, she [the principal] believed me. She investigated the situation based on information that I shared about the child. At no time did I feel unsupported. It reminded me of the way my parents would protect us as children. She used our trust to clear me.

In contrast, European American teachers only trusted their leaders of color in certain areas. European American teachers' trust of their principal was based on the issue and situation, type of information being shared, or experience with their principals. Due to the stereotypes (i.e., favored teachers of the same ethnic group, unequal distribution of resources and praise) that European American teachers held about their principals, it appeared that they only trusted their principals on areas of instructional programming. Over time, these European American teachers trusted their leaders because of their accomplishments and abilities. However, when their African American principals required that they become more responsive to students of color and use culturally relevant pedagogy, their trust level and support for their leaders decreased. European American teachers were uncomfortable addressing these ethnic or cultural issues with confidence and were troubled with how to respond to their principals' demands. One European American male teacher characterized his perspective on controversial issue avoidance as follows:

> I tend to keep quiet. I have opinions about how students of any color should be treated at my school. However, when you feel that your words may be misunderstood, you learn not to say anything. I think that this position makes me feel powerless. I am a good teacher and can teach students of any color.

Teachers of color noted their racial kinship with their principal that allowed them to feel comfortable sharing with their principal. In contrast, European American teachers stated they were uncomfortable in their exchanges with them because of their principals' ethnicity. The European American teachers believed that because they did not have some sense of bonding with their African American principals, they felt at ease in relating personal information to their principals. The European American teachers believed that by not sharing personal information about themselves, they maintained a higher level of trust with their principals. Because of the racial overtones, they limited their contacts with their principals to avoid possible retaliation. The European American teachers felt that if they maintained professional interactions their principals could not evaluate them on their racial beliefs. European American teachers wanted their principals to perceive them as a responsible member of the organization, yet they were uncomfortable with addressing issues of race. As a European American teacher summarized,

> As a white teacher here, you just have to show that you can be trusted ... prove your loyalty. She [the principal] has never lied to me or anyone else. I keep my personal life to myself. I think that this is better for everyone involved in this school.

Credibility with followers. The last area of image management examined was the leaders' credibility with followers. As Chemers and Murphy (1995) found, leaders of color faced credibility barriers with their diverse followers. Accordingly, in this study, African American and European American teachers perceived their principals' credibility differently (see Table 2). Because the African American teachers believed that only those leaders of color whose credentials far surpassed other European American leaders were selected for principalship, they viewed their African American principals as legitimate. This urban district had a poor record in promoting leaders of color to principals because rumors surfaced that the African American leaders were viewed as not possessing certain leadership characteristics that the European American leaders did. In contrast, European American teachers believed that their educational levels and capabilities defined their African American principals' credibility. However, some of the European American teachers voiced concern if their principals also were hired because of their race and not their credentials. (Although this concern arose in interviews, none of the European American teachers wanted to share their perceptions about it.)

The perceptions that teachers of color had about the credibility of their leaders of color were based on the principal's position in the organization and their work ethic. Because there were few leaders of color in this district, they viewed their principals' elevation to the top position as through hard work. Teachers of color characterized hard work as working past regular hours, solving problems of followers and community people, and gaining higher levels of professional education. Also, several teachers of color noted that promotion for a person of color within the district was due to their efforts and recognition as leaders by their European American colleagues. As a result, they concluded that promotions were race based, but strongly believed that they should not be. As one veteran teacher of color summed up her perception,

> My principal is from the same background as me. She knows what it is to be from a poor background like these kids. It just lets me know that someone from my racial background has been able to achieve the things that she has. Also, she does more because our culture expects more from our leaders. It's not because she is a token in a leadership position.

In contrast, the European American teachers gravitated toward accomplishment indicators as factors for a leader's advancement in the organization. In short, they believed that their principals earned their position through their credentials as had other European American principals. These credentials included the number of professional degrees, achievement awards, and personal standing in the community. As a result, the European American teachers viewed their African American principals' credibility as a reflection of their accomplishments in the organization. A fifth-year European American teacher summarized this collective view:

> She is very smart. She's changed this school through hard work and got us off the low-performing list. She deserves all of the credit. She has earned two college degrees and many awards for her efforts; no wonder she is a good leader. The more she does for this school, the more she will be recognized for her efforts. She deserves all of the applause.

Relationship Development

The second theme in Chemers's (1993) model for leading a diverse group of followers is relational development. This leadership theme focuses on the quality of the interpersonal relationships between the leader and followers (see Table 1). Both groups of teachers' responses were based on how they were able to establish personal relationships and positively interact with their principals (see Table 2). Exchanges between the leaders of color and both the African American and European American teachers were influenced by (a) motivation strategies, (b) accurate and fair evaluations of both groups of teachers, (c) establishing a comfort level, and (d) validation of teachers' work efforts.

Motivating followers. Motivating followers is characterized as the leader's interactions that promote or affect followers' active participation in pursuing organizational goals. As Chemers and Murphy (1995) found, the quality of the relationship between leader and followers affects followers' commitment to the organization as a whole. In this study, the teachers of color responded favorably to their principals' motivational efforts. They felt their principals' shared information, created a risk-taking environment, and promoted teacher leader opportunities as motivators for them. As a result, teachers of color felt that they had a strong relationship with their principals (see Table 2). In contrast, the European American teachers felt that their leaders' emphasis on them to be culturally relevant kept them committed to their school. These teachers believed that their principals expected them to have high expectations for students of color and ensure students performed well on standardized tests. As a result, European American teachers noted they were more responsive to the needs of students of color (see Table 2).

Teachers of color noted they were motivated by their principals' willingness to share valuable organizational information. Some of the teachers had been in similar schools with European American principals, but they did not feel important information was exchanged with them. By sharing information, the teachers of color perceived that their principals provided technical support for them to make effective instructional and programming decisions by themselves. As a result, they felt secure to seek technical information without hesitation, formulate innovative ideas, and participate in open discussions to solve problems. Also, because teachers of color felt that their principals promoted innovative practices, they felt comfortable taking risks. These leaders of color established the type of exchange that these teachers had not encountered in other schools. One teacher of color shared her perception about being motivated as follows:

> She [the principal] allows you to continually stretch your limits with her support and resources. Although some people mess up, she still

tells us to keep trying. She often says that a failure is an opportunity for future success. You can't help but keep trying for her.

Lastly, the teachers of color described how their principals created leadership opportunities for everyone in the school. Due to the racial affiliation, these teachers felt they were given greater freedoms with their principals. These leadership opportunities helped them to believe in their abilities to lead others on instructional and management issues. They felt that teacher–leaders were selected based on experience, special training, and recommendations from their peers. As a result, these leadership opportunities inspired them to take on additional school duties and challenging assignments, sometimes beyond their perceived limits. One teacher of color summed her view as follows:

Well, she makes you feel comfortable whenever you want to talk to her. She listens to your side of the story. You feel that you can share, you know, anything with her. She gives you good advice like a mother. And you feel that whatever you tell her will be held confidential. In return, you want to help her accomplish all the things that she wants to do for the school and the community.

In contrast, European American teachers' perceptions of their principals' motivating ability reflected a different view. They characterized their principals' ability to motivate them as "proving" their worth. This perception was characterized as their ability to use culturally relevant strategies to improve the achievement of students of color. This meant for European American teachers that they were motivated by their principals to be responsive to the success of students of color in the classroom. Some of the European American teachers felt if they "proved themselves" they were rewarded by the principals' individual attention and given opportunities to be elevated to leadership positions. Also, some believed that the press by their leaders of color to be culturally relevant and to have high expectations for students of color was an important motivator for them. One veteran European American teacher shared his thoughts:

I have been around this business a long time. He is very supportive and has an open-door policy. However, when I first started to work under him, I, like my White colleagues, felt that we had to prove ourselves in order to be considered okay. I thought that this was unfair. As I step back and look at it now, I think that I know why he does it. You have to show that you can be trusted and prove your loyalty to the school and kids.

Evaluation fairness. Another aspect of relationship building was the leader's ability to evaluate fairly followers' performances. Evaluation fairness is characterized by the leader's ability to accurately and objectively evaluate followers' performances per established standards and guidelines (Chemers & Murphy, 1995). In this study, both teachers of color and European American teachers mostly perceived assessments of their performances as fair. The teachers of color believed that their evaluations were based on their performance and ability to mutually exchange information about differences. However, the European American teachers felt they were held to different standards than the teachers of color. They expressed that if they were to receive good evaluations, they were expected to ensure fair treatment and equitable opportunities for students of color. As a result, European American teachers felt that they had to change their instructional methods to receive high performance ratings like their ethnic counterparts.

Teachers of color noted that their principals' fairness was in their ability to listen. During discussions about their evaluations, whether they agreed or disagreed with a particular indicator rating, they felt that their principals listened. As a result, they felt that they could talk about disagreements without fear of retaliation. Also, many of the teachers of color felt that because their students of color were successful, they could talk more freely with their principals. One teacher of color voiced a collective perspective regarding their principals' fairness:

> She sees everything in your classroom. She basically knows how you will be evaluated before she does it officially. After you get your results, she points out all of your strengths and documents where you can improve. If you disapprove of a rating, she goes to her notes and shows you why you received the rating. Also, she tells you that she is willing to help you improve. Since we have been together for such a long time, I just cannot help but trust her judgment and opinions with my evaluations.

European American teachers' perceptions of their principals' evaluation fairness varied somewhat from the teachers' of color responses. Although the European American teachers felt their principals were fair, they also believed there were underlying performance criteria they had to overcome. These hurdles were placed on them to be responsive to the diverse needs of students of color and to ensure their academic success. Most felt that they were being nudged to change from their traditional mode of teaching to a model that included culturally relevant pedagogy. One European American teacher characterized her perception as follows:

I was a new teacher some years ago. I could not understand why my ratings were not as high as I thought that they should be. One day, one of my White colleagues told me that I had to prove my teaching before "she" [the principal] would give me higher ratings. And once I proved myself, I didn't have to worry anymore. I respect her evaluations and tell new White teachers that it will be all right.

Most of the European American teachers rose to their principals' challenge of being culturally responsive. There were some European American teachers who expressed some disagreement about how their teaching was perceived and evaluated. As a result, two beliefs were expressed by those European American teachers who disagreed with their evaluations. One side believed that their low ratings resulted from their lack of success with students of color. The other side felt that poor evaluations were a result of personal conflicts with their African American principals. A fourth-year European American female teacher shared these comments:

You try to stay respectful and believe that she [the principal] is fair. However, you have a right to disagree even though your students didn't do well on one test. Your efforts should count for something. If it doesn't count for something, then I can't stay here. But I will try to change to meet the needs of my students.

Comfort level. A third aspect of relationship development is the leader's ability to exchange information or dialogue with their followers (Chemers & Murphy, 1995). Other researchers, such as Graen and Scandura (1987), found that followers who enjoy better relationships with their leaders have higher levels of task performance and job satisfaction. Teachers of color noted their "kinship" with their principals; thus, they developed a strong rapport with them. The European American teachers felt uncomfortable about discussing racial and personal issues. The veteran European American teachers noted that they had developed defense mechanisms to withdraw when racial or personal matters were addressed. The novice European American teachers felt comfortable only addressing instructional strategies with their principals. Also, many of the European American teachers expressed being left out in their exchanges with their principals because they did not have a racial connection to them. Because of their principals' ethnicity, the European American teachers did not feel comfortable sharing information and trusting their principals.

Teachers of color perceived that their principals provided time to exchange ideas and opportunities to talk. In many ways, there was a kinship between the teachers of color and their African American principals. This cultural alliance was important because it gave voice to these teachers and created opportunities for recruiting and retaining other teachers of color. This kinship allowed them to approach their principals with professional or private thoughts, new ideas, voice concerns, and ask for advice with ease. As a result, they felt secure in bringing innovative ideas to improve the academic or social climate of the school. Furthermore, they expressed how their comfort level continued to expand as their principals were more open to their ideas. As this quote indicates,

> We can talk to her [the principal] about anything. It can be professional or personal. Since I have been here, I have gone to her many times about personal family problems. She was there to listen. I know that it is not her job to be a counselor.

Veteran European American teachers believed that they felt at ease and confident in discussing educational issues with their principals. However, they voiced feeling uneasy during one-on-one exchanges regarding personal issues (i.e., family problems or peer conflicts) or controversial topics (i.e., ethnical or cultural differences). Their reasons for limiting their contact with their principal included being labeled as insensitive to students of color, peer conflicts with teachers of color, and possibly racially offending them. As a result, European American veteran teachers mostly evaded such situations or remained silent when race issues were addressed. A veteran European American teacher shared this view:

> I come to work everyday. I have learned to mind my own business and shared this view with others [European American teachers]. I found that my principal respects me, and I highly respect her. However, there is something that comes over me when I try to get to personal with her. I don't know what it is; it's just there. It may be because we are from different worlds and perspectives.

On the other hand, novice European American teachers stated that they did not discuss controversial or personal issues at their schools. These novice teachers conveyed that they only felt comfortable discussing peripheral instructional and social issues with their leaders. As a result, they used this technique to help them survive and reduce their anxiety in working with their principals. A novice European American teacher shared the following avoidance strategy regarding her African American principal:

> I am new around here. I do not want to get on anyone's bad side. Therefore, I watch what I say and keep my focus on my students. This way if a problem comes up that is controversial, I just retreat into my own room.

Another discomfort for both the veteran and novice European American teachers regarded their intergroup interactions with their principals. As members of the organization, they expressed feelings of being "left out" from daily interactions with their African American principals. They described observations about how their principals interacted with teachers of color in a friendlier way than with them. Such observations included the exchanging of jokes, sharing family stories and events, inviting each other to social events outside of school, and bonding as partners. As a result, their left out feelings made them feel uneasy in their exchanges with their principals and also influenced how they interacted with the teachers of color. As noted by this European American teacher,

> I sometime watch the interactions she [the principal] and the African American teachers have with each other. They share small talk about their families, appear to know what the other is thinking, or know each other's needs. Even when I am with an African American teacher friend that I trust, I feel uncomfortable talking about personal stuff. It's just hard to open up.

Validation of teachers' efforts. One area not found in Chemers's (1993) model was the European American teachers' need for validation. One conclusion may be that the European American teachers perceived that their African American principals did not recognize their individual work efforts (see Table 2). Further studies may need to be undertaken to understand how leaders of color validate their followers' work effort or if there are cultural differences in terms of praise or validation. Another issue may be that there are cultural differences in dissemination of praise or validation among different ethnic groups. Although the researcher originally was not analyzing how workers were validated, it continually arose only in European American respondents' interviews. Teachers of color described the level of praise from their principals as basically a "nonissue." Also, they felt they received "adequate" praise for their efforts in their school. As a result, the teachers of color believed that their effectiveness or commitment should not be judged based on individual achievements, but the success of their students.

In this study, *praise* was the term characterized by the European American teachers. The researcher made the decision to interchange the terms *praise* and *validation* for this study only. One aspect of praise and validation in this study was how the term related to gender, problems with praise, and the need for praise. In the area of gender, praise was not a cause–effect relationship for men in this study. European American men expressed that they did not need validation to continue their efforts on behalf of the organization. Although praise in any form was basically an acknowledgment of their efforts, the European American men did not seek it from their African American principals. However, the European American women believed that praise was crucial to further their commitment to the organizational goals and to further their own personal fulfillment at the school.

In particular, both the veteran and novice female teachers wanted to be recognized for their individual teaching performances, extracurricular activities, and team-building efforts. Because they felt they had "proven themselves" in the "eyes of their principals," they deserved individual rewards appropriate to their efforts. These teachers believed that validation of their work efforts would keep them committed and loyal to the organization and the leader. A novice European American female teacher characterized a collective perception about receiving praise:

> We are proving ourselves to her [the principal]. Many times we do a lot of great things. You may not be looking for praise for everything you do, but we need more from her. She just needs to do more.

A veteran European American female teacher voiced her perception slightly differently about receiving personal validation, as follows:

> This teaming thing is okay. I am used to it now. But sometimes your team members don't work as hard as you. Therefore, I think that I should receive praise for my individual accomplishments in the school. My students do well, their parents like me, and I can hold my head up high. I think that she should always look for ways to praise our efforts, don't you.

Findings from this study revealed that the leaders of color were not validating these European American teachers' work efforts. In contrast, the African Americans made no mention of this, nor did they expect to be validated. If they received praise and validation from their principals, it was received as an acknowledgment for efforts beyond the call of duty. However, the European American teachers viewed praise in a different context. They expressed that praise should be distributed mostly for individual efforts rather than for their group efforts. Therefore, they mostly connected their future efforts with the amount of praise received through their accomplishments or completed tasks in the organization.

A final focus in this section was the personal need for praise. The teachers of color were culturally socialized to believe that praise was not expected for their efforts. They conveyed that praise was an unexpected acknowledgment from someone. Also, it was undignified to seek praise for personal acknowledgment over the needs of others. On the other hand, European American female teachers mostly believed that praise was necessary to keep them committed and focused on organizational tasks. Without consistent recognition and rewards they would begin to question their loyalty to the organization, which could possibly affect their individual and team efforts. As a result, their skills and experience would be lost to the overall organizational mission.

Conclusions

Leadership and diversity are strongly connected if the organization is demographically and culturally diverse (Chen & Van Velsor, 1996). Based on the findings about organizational diversity, researchers have found that due to a person's socialization about others who are dissimilar to them, they tend to make value judgments, character assessments, and stereotypical assumptions. Therefore in schools, how do teachers of color and European American teachers perceive leaders of color in these contexts? The intent of this study was to ascertain perceptions about African American principals' leadership capacity in successful urban schools. Thus, results from this study could (a) expand the knowledge of leaders of color and the understanding of diverse followers; (b) help leaders of color to create an inclusive environment where all ethnic groups feel accepted; and (c) aid in understanding the role leaders of color play in the recruitment and retention of members of diverse ethnic groups.

Findings from this study revealed that African American principals' leadership in urban schools was perceived differently by their ethnically diverse followers (see Table 2). The teachers of color characterized their principals' leadership capacity as (a) leading as an ethnic example, (b) taking responsibility for moving forward the organizational work, (c) accomplishing tasks in the best interest of all, and (d) treating followers fairly. However, the European American teachers shared a somewhat different view of their African American principals' leadership. They expressed that their principals were (a) intellectually competent leaders because they possessed certain leadership characteristics, (b) obtained certain credentials, and (c) learned to be fair with them. In summary, teachers of color believed in their principals' leadership because of their ethnic kinship and organizational position, whereas the European American teachers believed that their principals had quantifiable accomplishments and professional interactions.

As perceived by both teacher groups, their leader's ethnicity had an impact on his or her leadership of the school. Although European American teachers could not quantify or qualify, they felt their principals' ethnicity affected their interactive relationships with them. The teachers of color perceived that their principals' ethnicity enhanced their commitment to stated goals and loyalty to the organization. As a result, teachers of color felt that the relationship bonds between them and their principals were like those of family members. Therefore, the efforts and comments by teachers of color strongly supported this familial approach by their leaders of color because they helped them to become successful in the organization.

Teachers of color seemed to view themselves as "parts of a whole" due to the success of their leaders of color. They described their comfort level with their African American principals as a "confessional." In other words, they could discuss any issue or topic with their principals without fear of retaliation. As a result, they felt comfortable sharing information with them about personal issues (i.e., family problems, relationship difficulties, advice on health) and professional matters (i.e., approaching a reluctant colleague, dealing with abusive parents).

On the other hand, the European American teachers perceived that ethnic affiliation had only a minor effect on their leaders' success in the organization and their comfort level with them. Although they felt that their African American principals' presence created an inclusive environment, other factors were more important to them. These elements included their principals' ability to obtain needed resources, receive awards for the organizations and themselves, and solve problems that affected their working conditions and comfort level. As a result, the European American teachers felt that trust between them and validation from their principals were essential to their continued commitment and progress in the organization.

Researchers have discovered that organizations must recruit and retain ethnically diverse leaders as a way to bring collaboration among the various ethnic groups. Findings from this study indicated that the management by leaders of color was perceived differently by teachers of color and by European American teachers. Although these differences seemed to be insignificant to several teachers from both groups, their impact has a tremendous effect on the recruitment of leaders of color to the organization. As mentioned earlier in this article, African American principals faced challenges in their leadership role and must be flexible in working with all ethnic groups. As noted by Banks (1991), leaders of color must be viewed as strong but not too strong. They must be viewed as competent but not too arrogant. They must be viewed as resourceful but in an equitable manner. Also, they must be viewed as the authority figure yet approachable in the organization. As a result and despite these daily challenges, they must prove leadership capabilities in a calm and affirmative way.

With this knowledge, leaders of color must be recruited not only for their leadership characteristics and performance (Chen & Van Velsor, 1996) but also for the different perspectives they bring to the leadership position. Also, diverse leaders would bring different insights about ethnic histories, cultural practices, and alternative ways to obtain and use organizational resources. As a result, leaders of color would be valued as an integral, trusted, and equal member of the leadership team.

Finally, *leadership diversity*, a term used by Morrison (1992), can be achieved if those who were traditionally locked out are allowed to participate in the leadership of the organization. As Chen and Van Velsor (1996) indicated, diversity leaders must be allowed to be people developers. With this "empowerment of followers" aspect of their duties, diverse leaders have a special responsibility to create conditions and environments to help everyone in the organization reach his or her highest potential. Although this aspect of leadership has not been widely used in diverse organizations, the time for its implementation has come as our organizations become more diverse and the need for leaders of color is ever so great.

References

Banks, C. (1991). *City school superintendents: Their career patterns, traits, and perceptions of leadership and managerial skills and style*. Unpublished doctoral dissertation, Seattle University.

Bass, B. (1985). *Leadership and performance beyond expectations*. New York: Free Press.

Boyatzis, R. E. (1998). *Transforming qualitative information: Thematic analysis and code development*. Thousand Oaks, CA: Sage.

Chemers, M. (1993). An integrative theory of leadership. In M. M. Chemers & R. Ayman (Eds.), *Leadership theory and research: Perspective and directions* (pp. 293–319). San Diego, CA: Academic.

Chemers, M., & Murphy, S. (1995). Leadership and diversity in groups and organizations. In M. M. Chemers, S. Oskamp, & M. A. Costanzo (Eds.), *Diversity in organizations* (pp. 157–188). Thousand Oaks, CA: Sage.

Chen, C., & Van Velsor, E. (1996). New directions for research and practice in diversity leadership. *Leadership Quarterly, 7*, 285–302.

Conger, J., & Kanungo, R. (1988). Behavioral dimensions of charismatic leadership. In J. Conger & R. Kanungo (Eds.), *Charismatic leadership: The elusive factor in organizational effectiveness* (pp. 78–97). San Francisco: Jossey-Bass.

Conrad, C. (1982). Grounded theory: An alternative approach in higher education. *Review of Higher Education, 5*, 259–269.

Cox, T. (1994). *Cultural diversity in organizations: Theory, research, and practice.* San Francisco: Berrett-Koehler.

Delpit, L. (1995). *Other people's children: Cultural conflict in the classroom.* New York: New Press.

Foster, M. (1995). African-American teachers and culturally relevant pedagogy. In J. Banks & C. Banks (Eds.), *Handbook on resource of multicultural education* (pp. 570–581). New York: Macmillan.

Graen, G., & Scandura, T. (1987). Toward a psychology of dyadic organizing. In B. M. Staw & L. L. Cummings (Eds.), *Research in organizational behavior* (Vol. 9, pp. 175–207). Greenwich, CT: JAI.

Hollander, E. (1964). *Legitimacy, power, and influence: A perspective on relational features of leadership.* New York: Oxford University Press.

Linden, R., Wayne, S., & Stillwell, D. (1993). A longitudinal study on the early development of leader-member exchanges. *Journal of Applied Psychology, 78*, 662–674.

Lomotey, K. (1989). *African-American principals: School leadership and success.* New York: Greenwood.

Merriam, S. B. (1988). *Case study research in education: A qualitative approach.* San Francisco: Jossey-Bass.

Morrison, A. (1992). *The new leaders: Guidelines on leadership diversity in America.* San Francisco: Jossey-Bass.

Pollard, D. (1997). Race, gender, and educational leadership: Perspectives from African-American principals. *Educational Policy, 11*, 353–374.

Sizemore, B. (1986). The limits of the Black superintendency: A review of the literature. *Journal of Educational Equity and Leadership, 6*, 180–208.

Triandis, H. (1993). The contingency model in cross-cultural perspective. In M. M. Chemers & R. Ayman (Eds.), *Leadership theory and research: Perspectives and directions* (pp. 167–188). San Diego, CA: Academic.

Valverde, S. (1987). A comparative study of Hispanic high school dropouts and graduates: Why do some leave school early and some finish? *Education in Urban Society, 19*, 320–329.

African American Leaders' Perceptions of Intergroup Conflict

Jean A. Madsen
Texas A & M University

Reitumetse Obakeng Mabokela
Michigan State University

>Educational organizations that reflect a diversity of class, gender, socioeconomic status, and nationality establish a complex set of interactions that have implications for how groups are formed. This article examines how African American principals perceive intergroup conflict and acknowledges their leadership concerns in working with European American participants in desegregated suburban schools. Findings from this study revealed these "color-conscious" leaders were cultural integrators and consensus builders who had acquired an understanding of diversity of groups and were able to establish leader–member trust. Whether due to their ethnic backgrounds or leadership capabilities, these African American principals often struggled with how to respond to the needs of both minority and majority groups in dealing with intergroup conflict.

Requests for reprints should be sent to Jean A. Madsen, Educational Administration and Human Resource Development 4226 TAMU Texas A & M University, College Station, TX 77843.

J. A. Madsen and R. O. Mabokela

Leaders of color who interact with multiple groups must deal with a followership that may not be supportive (Chemers, 1993). Research reveals that followers' perceptions of a leader of color are often checked against prototypes. That is, leaders of color undergo scrutiny to determine their capabilities and professional contributions. Consequently, there are concerns about how minorities in majority organizations are promoted to leadership positions. Cox (1994) contended that in organizations, properties of intergroup conflict will influence how the leader and majority and minority members will perceive and respond to each other. Therefore, this article examines how African American school leaders (assistant principals) in suburban desegregated schools perceive and negotiate sources of intergroup conflict with their European American school participants. The researchers specifically seek to (a) understand how African American assistant principals perceive intergroup conflict as it affects their ability to lead and (b) acknowledge the challenges that African American school administrators face in leading a predominantly European American group of school participants.

Theoretical Framework

Intergroup Relations in Organizations

According to Alderfer and Smith (1982), many organizations are comprised of two types of groups: identity groups and organization groups. An identity group is one whose members share common biological characteristics; participate in equivalent historical experiences, at times subjected to certain social forces; and hold similar worldviews (Alderfer & Smith, 1982; Nkomo & Cox, 1996). When people enter organizations, they bring with them their identity groups, which are based on variables such as ethnicity, sex, age, and family background. An organization group is one in which members share common organizational positions, participate in common work experiences, and have similar organizational views (Alderfer & Smith, 1982; Nkomo & Cox, 1996). An important factor in understanding intergroup relations in organizations is that membership in identity groups is not independent from membership in organizational groups. Thus, certain organizational groups tend to be filled by members of particular identity groups.

Intergroup theory contains a complex set of interactions for understanding the effects of diversity of identities in the workplace. Identity group and organizational membership are seen as highly related in their effects on social relations in organizations (Nkomo & Cox, 1996). When people of different subgroups interact with each other, there is increased potential for intergroup conflict (Ayman, 1993). Such conflict is often viewed as negative because it requires majority workers to adjust their patterns of interaction with minority counterparts. The leader strongly influences relations among groups, establishes the emotional climate of the workplace, determines how roles are structured, and plays a pivotal role in how intergroup conflict is addressed within the organization (Alderfer, 1977).

Intergroup theory, leadership, and diversity are three areas that are invariably connected. Mainstream leadership theories view leadership as intrapersonal (personality characteristics) and interpersonal (exchange between leaders and followers) but rarely intergroup. When intergroup interactions are implied, the focus is on the organizational group rather than on identity groups. Thus, in traditional hierarchical organizations composed of homogeneous groups, a leader may effectively lead a group because the values, needs, and expectations of the followers are similar. Therefore, if leaders do not recognize the legitimacy of social identity groups, they will not effectively deal with issues of gender, race, and other demographic dimensions.

In contrast, diversity leadership perspectives look beyond leaders and followers and organizational identities to social, racial, and cultural issues that are outside organizational boundaries, but affect leader–member interactions inside the organization (Chen & Van Velsor, 1996). Thus, intergroup theory in leadership research may provide a better understanding of the dynamics of diversity leadership. Diversity issues highlight the complexities of subconscious or unconscious psychological forces that affect people's perceptions of leaders of color (Chen & Van Velsor, 1996). Consequently, the result of misconceptions of majority followers is that leaders of color face an uphill climb in leading an organization. The issue becomes more complex due to the interdependence of leader and follower when the leader is a person of color.

Sources of Intergroup Conflict

Research on intergroup theory in organizations has identified a number of characteristics that create opposing interests among groups. These sources of intergroup conflict are not dependent on particular groups or the specific setting where the relationships occur (Alderfer & Smith, 1982). The analysis of intergroup relations is in part the study of power relations and the analysis of conflict among groups. Unequal power in intergroup relationships occurs when individuals who share a common condition induced by actions of a high-power group form an association as a way to improve their status (Alderfer, 1977). Relations among groups may determine the effectiveness of a group in achieving its objectives (Alderfer, 1977).

In the context of intergroup conflict, there are conditions that influence how the leader and majority and minority groups will react to each other (Cox, 1994). A leadership model that recognizes the effects of power differences, inequality, and conflict that originates from both identity and organizational groups will assist leaders in negotiating, creating consensus, and building alliances among groups (Chen & Van Velsor, 1996). Various researchers have identified multiple sources of conflict and refer to how one condition of discord seems to affect another (Alderfer, Alderfer, Tucker, & Tucker, 1980; Alderfer & Smith, 1982; Cox, 1994). These properties include incompatible goals, competition for resources, cultural differences, power differences, conformity versus identity, group boundaries, affective patterns, cognitive formations, and leadership behavior. These properties are often the cause of tensions between organizational and identity groups. (See Figure 1 for definitions of intergroup properties.)

In educational settings, intergroup theory applies to school participants because of the nature of the organizational context among groups. Because schools reflect the diversity, class, gender, socioeconomic status, and nationality of their students, it results in a complex set of interactions for how groups are formed. Much is written on how majority schools maintain a strong organizational culture through the process of selecting teachers. In schools, a dominant culture exists that imposes beliefs about appropriate ways of educating children. According to Lewis (2001), the fostering of a "color-blind" ideology allows most teachers to see themselves as racially neutral and deserving of their own success and not responsible for the exclusion of others. Consequently, an organizational culture exists that is maintained but is not reflective of its diverse student body. Thus, the theoretical framework of intergroup theory is useful in understanding sources of conflict that occur in suburban desegregated schools due to issues of diversity and the leader's ability to establish an inclusive school culture.

Methodology

Data Collection

This qualitative study used intensive open-ended and follow-up interviews for data collection. Due to the related experiences of these participants, it resulted in a single case analysis. For this study, a case study is defined as a single entity, a unit of similar participants within the bounded

Competing Goals: Differences among majority and nonmajority workers result in competing goals that are influenced by norms, goal priorities, and work styles among and between these groups (Cox, 1994).

Competition for Resources: Allocation of resources that are influenced by embedded organizational issues such as acknowledgment of group identities in regulating jobs, training priorities, and expansion of resources (Cox, 1994).

Cultural Differences: Cultural differences between group members of different groups occur due to misunderstanding and misperceptions (Cox, 1994).

Power Differences: Majority groups hold advantages over minority groups in the power structure of the organization. Intergroup hostility between groups results in a disagreement over the redistribution of power. Minority group density in organizations poses a threat to the existing power structure and provides an opportunity for those who are powerless. The types of resources that can be obtained and used differ among groups (Alderfer & Smith, 1982; Cox, 1994).

Conformity versus Identity Affirmation: The tension between majority and minority group members over the preservation of minority group identity (Cox, 1994).

Group Boundaries: Both physical and psychological group boundaries determine group membership. Transactions among groups are regulated by variations in the permeability of the boundaries (Alderfer & Smith, 1982).

Affective Patterns: The severity of intergroup conflict relates to the polarized feelings among the groups. Group members split their feelings so that positive feelings are associated with their group and negative feelings are associated with other groups (Alderfer & Smith, 1982).

Cognitive Formations: Due to group boundaries, power differences, and affective patterns, group members develop their own language, influence members' perceptions of subjective and objective criteria of other groups and work efforts, and transmit propositions about other groups in relation to their own group members (Alderfer & Smith, 1982).

Leadership Behavior: The group leader reflects the boundaries of groups and how they will interact. Members of a similar group reflect power differences, affective patterns, and cognitive formations of their group in relation to the other group. The role of the leader in a network of intergroup relations determines the intensification of intergroup conflict (Alderfer, 1977; Alderfer & Smith, 1982).

Figure 1. Properties of Intergroup Conflict

context of suburban desegregated schools (Merriam, 1988). Several African American leaders in suburban schools were contacted regarding their willingness to participate in this study. It is important to note that the representation of African Americans and other ethnic minorities in leadership positions was very low, and in some districts there were no minorities at all. Thus, the sample consists of 4 African American assistant principals from suburban school districts who were interviewed on two separate occasions. The primary objective of these interviews was to understand

J. A. Madsen and R. O. Mabokela

African American school leaders' responses to intergroup conflict that occurred as a result of cultural incongruities between them and their European American counterparts in these contexts.

Data Analysis

We used a qualitative thematic strategy of data analysis to organize and categorize the data. This inquiry process led to a single-case level of analysis in which the findings were aggregated to incorporate a thematic approach. This process allowed important themes and categories to emerge inductively from the data across cases. The findings from the assistant principals' interviews were clustered by key themes across schools and single cases. The researchers used the prior-research-driven approach to identify themes and coding process (Boyatzis, 1998). To establish the reliability of these assistant principals' perceptions of intergroup conflict, the data were analyzed using what Conrad (1982) called a *constant comparative method.* This coding process was constructed by comparing the assistant principals' perceptions with sources of intergroup conflict to determine how these principals managed their schools. The findings from this study closely followed the themes identified in sources of conflict between identity and organizational groups. (See Figure 1 for intergroup properties and Figure 2 for themes that emerged from the analysis of intergroup properties from this study.)

As a way to bring about a collective interpretation in the data analysis, the researchers perceived it was important for readers to understand the complexities in collecting and analyzing cross-cultural research. Stanfield (1993) argued that there are ethical considerations in researching people of color and their contexts. Because of cultural and class and gender differences, the collection and analysis of data require a special sensitivity about these discrepancies. Furthermore, researchers in mainstream disciplines rarely reflect on how their racial identities influence their interpretations of data (Stanfield, 1993). Cross-cultural interpretations of data must be sensitive to issues of race because this may prohibit an appropriate interpretation of the findings.

The interpretation of the data was a joint effort between a European American and a colleague of color to ensure a sound cross-cultural analysis. Developing more inclusive ways to analyze data entails that minority group members have insights about and interpretations of their experiences that are likely different than European American scholars (Andersen, 1993). This combined analysis was to ensure the validity and reliability of this qualitative study. In this cross-cultural analysis, each researcher

Incompatible Goals: Differences among majority and nonmajority workers result in competing goals that are influenced by norms, goal priorities, and work styles among and between these groups (Cox, 1994).

Group Boundaries and Cultural Differences: Cultural differences between group members of different groups occur due to misunderstandings and misperceptions that are related to the different worldviews of culture groups (Cox, 1994). Group boundaries are both the physical and psychological determinants of group boundaries used to determine group membership. Transactions among groups are regulated by variations in the permeability of the boundaries (Alderfer & Smith, 1982).

Power Differences: Majority groups hold advantages over minority groups in the power structure of the organization. The organization's culture that is shaped by societal culture and the organization's power holders determines the norms and values that define the power relations among groups in the organization (Ragins, 1995). Intergroup hostility between groups results in disagreement over the redistribution of power. Minority group density in organizations poses a threat to the existing power structure and provides an opportunity for those who are powerless. The types of resources that can be obtained and used differ among groups (Alderfer & Smith, 1982; Cox, 1994).

Leadership Behavior: The group leader and other group representatives reflect the boundaries of groups and how they will interact. Members of a similar group reflect power differences, affective patterns, and cognitive formations of their group in relation to the other group. The role of the leader in a network of intergroup relations determines the intensification of intergroup conflict (Alderfer, 1977; Alderfer et al., 1980; Alderfer & Smith, 1982).

Figure 2. Emergent Themes of Intergroup Conflict

analyzed and coded the data separately to protect its trustworthiness. To establish reliable and trustworthy interpretation of the findings, the researchers engaged in discussions about the coding differences in the cross-cultural interpretations of these participants' experiences (Merriam, 1988). Furthermore, there was a consistency of judgment among the researchers to determine code development and its application to data analysis (Boyatzis, 1998).

Data Sources

Districts and schools. This study took place in suburban districts that were participating in the city's metropolitan desegregation plan. The schools for this study were situated in multiple districts that were extensions of the more affluent metropolitan region. These districts were identified as having the most desirable elementary and secondary schools in the area. Although these districts were recognized for their academic quality and abundant resources, the neighboring inner-city schools did not share similar expectations. Consequently, inner-city students, the majority of whom were African American, participated in the voluntary desegregation program. An overwhelming number of the students and teachers in these suburban and desegregated schools were European American, with a growing number of students of color and even fewer teachers and administrators of color. Discussions with school administrators from districts participating in the voluntary desegregation plan indicated that they attempted to hire teachers of color without much success.

The schools that participated in this research project were in suburban school districts. These schools accepted approximately 15% of the African American students from the court-mandated desegregation program. The proportion of teachers of color in these districts was less than 4%.

Assistant principals. In the initial design of the study, the researchers planned to include principals and assistant principals in the interviews. However, there were no principals of color in the participating school districts. Thus, we interviewed all of the African American assistant principals from these suburban schools districts. Out of the 4 African American assistant principals, there were 3 men and 1 woman. Three of the participants were at the high school level, and the fourth (a man) was based at an elementary school. All of the participants had approximately 3 years of experience as assistant principals in their schools.

To gain a clearer understanding of these assistant principals' leadership, specifically, how they managed issues of diversity in the workplace, it is important to understand how their cultural backgrounds informed their leadership practices. Many of these participants had similar experiences while attending integrated schools at both the public school and university level. Due to their upbringing, education, and general life experiences, these African American leaders all seemed to develop an empathetic orientation in meeting the needs of all their school participants. This awareness, mixed with their own experiences and understanding, resulted in these school administrators developing a sense of tolerance in the area of human relations. They were able to understand the dilemmas that both people of color and European Americans face in dealing with cultural differences among groups and their role in minimizing these dissimilarities.

Roger Winter[1] grew up in an urban neighborhood and attended an integrated school until the fifth grade. He shared that in elementary school he was academically successful because the competition in his classes kept him focused on his studies. On completion of his elementary

---

[1] The names of the assistant principals used in this article are fictitious.

schooling, he was bused to a predominantly homogeneous European American school. During his years in high school, he experienced positive interactions and friendships with European American students. On graduation, he pursued his baccalaureate studies at a predominantly European American university. He studied journalism in college and became a sports writer for a local paper after graduation. After several years, he became "tired of this position." In his quest to "give back and work with African American children," Mr. Winter explored the possibility of coaching or substitute teaching. However, he was unable to secure a position in these areas. A personnel director recruited Mr. Winter to teach in a suburban school district. After teaching high school English for approximately 6 years, he was invited to apply for an administrator position in which he would be responsible for student management. Although he has played an important role to assist African American students navigate the maze of desegregated schooling, Mr. Winter expressed concerns about his own future in the district, especially opportunities for promotion.

Ralph Green was the only elementary assistant principal participating in this study. He received his elementary and high school education from mostly European American schools. After completing high school, Mr. Green joined the military, remaining there for 4 years. After his military experience, he attended a historically African American institution, where he received his teacher preparation training. Mr. Green began his teaching career in his current suburban school district. He taught in the district for 12 years before he was invited to apply for an assistant principal position at another school within the district. Mr. Green's scope of responsibilities includes student discipline, staff development, and community outreach. Like the other participants, he hopes to be an elementary principal in the near future.

Another participant, David Main, attended one of the most recognized preparatory high schools in the city. After completing high school, he attended a predominantly European American university at which he acquired his teacher preparation training. After his graduation from the university, Mr. Main applied for a teaching position at several suburban districts. He eventually took a position with one of the most prestigious suburban districts. After 2 years of teaching, he completed his master's degree in school administration. Although Mr. Main characterized himself as an excellent teacher, his ultimate goal was to be a school administrator. Therefore, after 3 years of teaching, he made the decision to leave the classroom. He interviewed in another suburban district for an assistant principal position at the high school level. Mr. Main was offered the position, which he has held for 2 years. He believes the principal at his high school has become his mentor.

The female assistant principal, Maxine Boyd, grew up in the rural south and attended mostly segregated schools. Ms. Boyd explained that she never had a White teacher until she entered college. She believes that African American teachers were important for her success and attributes their support to her aspiration to be a teacher. She attended a historically African American college in which she received her baccalaureate degree in teaching. After college graduation, she taught for 2 years in a rural community but soon became weary of teaching in a poverty-stricken area. She followed her family members to this city as part of the northern "Black migration." She obtained a teaching position within the city's schools and ascended through the ranks to eventually become an administrator. When the city implemented a policy that all administrators had to reside within the city limits (where she did not live), Ms. Boyd took a position in the suburban schools after 25 years of working in urban schools. She accepted a high school assistant principal position with a highly recognized suburban district. At the time of this study, Ms. Boyd had been in this position for 3 years. She noted that in her current administrative position, she spent most of her time with the "deseg" children who transferred to her district from city schools. Ms. Boyd struggled with how other administrators perceived her. She believed that there was an expectation that she was responsible for the African American students in her school. Although she enjoyed her role in the school, she often became tired of the stereotypes that confronted her on a daily basis. Of all of the participants, she noted the strains of feeling "out of place," yet needing to be there for the African American students.

Findings

An analysis of the assistant principals' perceptions and its relation to their leadership revealed four themes that were recognized as properties of intergroup conflict. These thematic interpretations included (a) incompatible goals among the assistant principals in leading the various school constituents; (b) problems of group boundaries and cultural differences in how they were perceived and their experiences with European American teachers' cultural differences; (c) power differences and how it influenced their interactions with teachers, parents, and other school administrators; and (d) the development of a color-conscious leadership in working with European American and African American teachers. (See Figures 1 and 2 for descriptions of intergroup conflict and themes.)

Incompatible Goals

In dealing with issues of diversity, various groups within a given organization may develop incompatible goals, which result in intergroup tensions. The data analysis revealed these school administrators struggled in their leadership with how to respond to incompatible goals between themselves and European American school participants. It was apparent that these school administrators were unable to shift the mind set of their school participants to accept issues of diversity in these schools. The incompatibility of goals and subsequent tensions for these school leaders emanated in the following areas: (a) the lack of commitment by their school participants to recruit teachers of color; (b) the lack of focus on the importance of diversity for both the African American and European American students; (c) their place as role models for both African American and European American students; and (d) the need for the assistant principals to prove their own worth within their schools.

The African American school leaders noted incompatible goals in their schools' lack of commitment to hire teachers of color. They eloquently expressed the importance that teachers of color played in the lives of all the students. Yet they met with resistance in their efforts to move their schools in this direction. These school administrators stated that their district often told them that they could not find "qualified minority" candidates. The male participants at both the elementary and secondary level noted that there was no district commitment at all to recruit teachers of color. Most agreed that none of their districts had identified specific strategies especially for minority teacher recruitment. It appeared that if people of color did apply, they were always met with a degree of hesitancy. The participants also noted that their districts were unclear on how to recruit for teachers of color, yet made little effort to assess the strategies they were using. This meant that personnel directors only went to teacher education programs at predominantly White universities and did not consider recruiting at historically African American institutions.

Of all the participants, Mr. Green was the most vocal in his attempts to get his district to recruit teachers of color. Mr. Green stated that when positions were advertised, he often identified several "qualified candidates" of color. However, he believed that his district put them through such intense scrutiny that they lost many candidates. Thus, he often was disappointed when he would review how many teachers of color were hired given the large numbers of available teaching positions. As he stated,

> We approached our district with a list of minority newspapers, black colleges and of all the black fraternal organizations to recruit. Well, this

year I made phone calls to minority candidates from the HBCUs. Of the eight who applied, only one was hired. Why weren't the others hired? I mean they [principals in other schools] made the minority applicants go four or five times for interviews before they were hired. It's discriminatory. They have not made a commitment to hiring Black, minority people. They don't like to hear it, but I'll tell them that. I am constantly reminding them of that. I think if they had a choice, they wouldn't hire them at all.

The female African American assistant principal, Ms. Boyd, had a different perspective on her district's hiring practices for teachers of color. She believed that her district's commitment to hire teachers of color was in part due to the "vocal" African American parents who lived in the district. She believed it was an "appeasement" factor, in which administrators provided "lip service" but never changed their personnel practices. When the district did hire teachers of color, she believed they were hired only to teach "safe subjects" such as music and vocational classes. She also noted that her district was hesitant to hire teachers from the city schools because they "brought too much baggage" with them. As she noted,

This is a community where the minority population is growing. This is a community that is vocal. I have seen appeasement. I have seen minorities hired in areas that are nonthreatening such as the fine arts, vocational classes, or in one instance, we have one at the lower level in foreign language. Of course, none of them at the high school level. They feel that a Black coming in from the city brings certain baggage. This is just my perception, no one has verbalized this. They feel that Blacks from the city talk a certain way that wouldn't be acceptable with kids here. The community is very involved and there is a lot of pressure on who is hired and who is not. I have seen Black teachers come and go here.

Another area of incompatibility was in their schools' and districts' commitment to issues of diversity, their lack of understanding African American students' needs, and the compelling need to hire "role models" for these students. All of the participants believed that they always had to make issues of diversity and the focus on African American students a priority. All of the male African American participants stated the importance of having "Black males" at the school to assist in promoting positive images for their male African American students. However, for Mr. Main at the high school level, he was more frustrated because he believed his presence as the "school's Black male" often jeopardized his relations with these students. Although he was able to negotiate effectively with the other African American students, he felt the distinct risk of alienating the other school participants. However, like the other participants, he felt a strong sense of conscience in needing to reach out and help the students of color, as this quote notes:

> Most of the African American students here are in the basic level courses. They are perceived to be the behavioral problems of the school. They are looked at as the kids who are not willing to deal with assimilation, that is the perception. I am talking in generalities. The problem is at the high school level there is not much I can do at this point. I have been asked, being in suburban districts for the past five years, to save Black boys. I think what happens is people see me work with black boys who are on the right track and I am able to influence where those kids are going.

Although Ms. Boyd noted the importance of "role models" as well, she also was concerned about the lack of student activities for the African American students to promote a sense of cultural identity. She believed that not only are role models important, but that African American students need additional support through school activities and special historical events. When it comes to Black History Month, she was the only person who willingly accepted this responsibility. As she noted,

> There is a lack of role models here. Role models stimulate self-esteem. Self-esteem enhances learning. It is not that a Black teacher or a White teacher can teach better. It is that a child sees someone who looks like them. They have a club [for African American students] here that brings in programs throughout the year. I am the only one who does things for the Black students here. During Black History Month, if I did not do anything, no one would. No one here knows what to do for the Black students here.

Another area of incompatibility for these African American leaders was their own feelings of self-conflict. In dealing with multiple cultural identities, these participants struggled with the complexity of race and its implications on their ability to lead. They often noted that their legitimacy was questioned concerning whether they were going to be loyal to school participants' collective interests or promote an ambivalent relationship with the African American students. Although they attempted to project an image highly consistent with their European American participants, they also were conflicted over how to respond to and be perceived by African American students.

Most of the participants felt that their color and its meaning became problematic in being promoted to principal. The African American leaders were cognizant of the fact that they had to avoid compromising themselves, yet had to negotiate the organizational ladder of being promoted. Mr. Green and Mr. Winter noted that their districts were not willing to promote "Blacks" into principalship. They believed that majority school participants (although unacknowledged) viewed them as cultural brokers who bridged the gap between the African American students and the district. These African American principals were valued for their ability to sensitize their European American colleagues about racial matters. Therefore, because of their importance in enlightening school participants on these issues and because there were too few African Americans in these positions, they became at risk for being promoted. In essence, they felt that just coming in and working hard and waiting to be promoted was not enough. They constantly had to fight stereotypes about their professional abilities. As noted,

> The superintendent brought in all these people, White females, whom he hired. Even though you know you are well regarded by teachers and parents, you can't get hired. And when you go to these district meetings, I am always wondering if I measure up. Do I measure up? So there's always this measuring your self against those yard sticks. Because you're always assuming that others are measuring you with that stick too. We go to these meetings and there are thousands of school administrators and only five Blacks. It just makes me wonder.

As cultural brokers, in working with both students of color and European American students, they wanted to be perceived as administrators who were more central to the mission of the school. Yet, they found themselves having to balance the intergroup conflict that occurred with the within group and between group processes in how they handled discipline with both the European American and African American students. Mr. Main stated that he was caught up in how he disciplined the students at his high school. On the one hand, his European American students perceived him as a "token" who was not fair in his discipline practices. Yet, the African American students thought he was harder on them. As he noted,

> I view myself as an advocate for Black students. I have to be. I also view my self as a role model for (European American) students who may be fearful in dealing with Black males. No other school administrator needs to view themselves in that way. I think those are two spe-

cial things I need to keep in mind. I need to be an advocate for Black students and if I don't do it, nobody else will. But I also need to be fair to all my students here.

Cultural Differences and Group Boundaries

Cultural differences that occur in the workplace may result in tensions among groups. Due to cultural differences, group boundaries are manifested where the majority group makes decisions on what is acceptable and establishes the norms and expectations. Findings from this study revealed that due to cultural differences, there were conflicts between the African American school administrators and European American school participants. These cultural differences were manifested in two ways. They became apparent in how (a) various school constituents perceived these leaders and (b) the assistant principals interacted with teachers about their instructional practices and the expectations and stereotypes they held about African American students.

All of the participants expressed "image management" concerns. Chemers and Murphy (1995) noted that when persons of color enter a leadership position in a mostly homogenous organization, they often face misperceptions by followers who question their effectiveness as leaders. Because followers' perceptions are susceptible to bias and distortion, it becomes important to recognize that trust and competency will influence the leader's ability to get followers to reach goal attainment. Thus, these assistant principals felt that due to negative perceptions held by their European American colleagues, they often spent much time and energy having to socially construct their roles to focus on one-on-one leader–member relationships of trust and reciprocity.

In some ways, Mr. Green at the elementary school noted his image management concerns more than his secondary counterparts. He spent a disproportionate amount of time explaining his leadership decisions to his European American colleagues. As he lamented,

> There was a conception when I was hired that they had to hire someone Black. There's no doubt in my mind that the committee held stereotypes about me. In terms of parents, I had no problems, because they knew I was serious. But the staff, I had conflict. They were pretty arrogant about me being in here.

The other participants noted similar reactions by their school participants. However, they noted the amount of time they had to spend in developing an inclusive relationship. This meant being open-minded in their personal and work-related actions to reduce the anxiety and uncertainty among school participants. In being inclusive, they believed they gained the respect of staff, which then allowed them to address cultural differences. In many ways, these participants felt they were often misperceived and encapsulated in certain roles. Ms. Boyd in particular noted her struggles in working with school participants. As she explained,

> Demanding respect for my position, having to prove myself that I am capable of this job is always in my mind. Having to work and at the same time watch out of the corner of my eye so that they will not sabotage my efforts. Or set me up for failure. I am making sure that I am not labeled as a disciplinarian, because a Black administrator can be labeled as a disciplinarian. That means you don't have any smarts, just know how to make kids behave. It is not a complimentary position.

These participants noted that part of their leadership role was to work with European American teachers about their own cultural differences with the African American students. These leaders of color cited the important role they played in "turning around" teachers about their pedagogical practices and instructional decisions. Again at the elementary level, these discussions with European American teachers were always at the forefront of Mr. Green's leadership. He noted that he often assisted European American teachers with how to interact with African American parents and encouraged them to have high expectations for students of color. He would not let these teachers operate on a deficit model in working with the students of color. As he noted,

> We would at times have African American kids who came in from the city, who were at times dirty. Teachers tended to push them away. And the kids can read it, and I hate teachers for that. So, therefore, for these children it is how they are perceived or viewed. These teachers have a lot to learn coming in here from their White middle class homes and cultural expectations. They are teaching in the unknown with those kids from different backgrounds. They just haven't learned how to bring those kids to where they should be. In other words, they pity them, you know poor little guy. This is what I work with.

The other participants at the high school level focused more on how cultural differences manifested themselves in how children of color were tracked into their high school programs. These participants noted that European American teachers perceived African American students as inferior because of their language. As a result, the students were disproportionately placed in the lower, nonacademic tracks. As Mr. Winter noted,

> We use a test in the eighth grade. The African American students are placed in certain tracks. More than likely those kids remain in those tracks. It is only if parents challenge the tracking does something get done. The majority of White students go into the upper tracks and our minority students are at the lower tracks. When they (African American students) come to us they are in the basics track. Only 7% are in the upper tracks.

Ms. Boyd also noted the intergroup conflict of getting European American participants to change their cultural beliefs about African Americans. She believed these teachers' "color blindness" resulted in them not addressing the racial realities that surrounded them. She asserted that the European American teachers' stereotypes about African Americans were so embedded that it would be difficult to change these beliefs, as she noted:

> You have people here who know nothing of the African American culture. Nor do they wish to learn. And you still have people there who will always say I am not reflecting on where they come from. I always say they have a South African mentality. You will always have them thinking that Blacks are inferior. They can be really smart Black children, but they are still Black so therefore, they are inferior.

Power Differences

Power differences between majority and minority members of an organization are the most problematic intergroup conflict conditions. Individuals with power define the organization's culture, determine which groups get power, and define the very nature of power. However, for leaders of color in managerial positions, they often reported having less job discretion and reported feeling less accepted than White managers (Greenhaus, Parasuraman, & Wormley, 1990). Ethnic differences between leader and followers may result in exchanges that may be detrimental to the organization's goals (Chemers & Murphy, 1995).

All of the participants noted that due to their positions of authority, they often grappled with how participants responded to their leadership. Due to these power struggles, each participant noted how certain school groups challenged his or her leadership. The power differences were manifested in two ways: (a) European American teachers' dismissal of the administrators' authority to change their instructional practices for students of color and (b) European American teachers' and other administrators' misconceptions of the assistant principals as "tokens" with little real power.

At the elementary level, Mr. Green noted that his power differences were more pronounced in his dealings with the European American teachers. He believed his role as instructional leader was to make teachers who were not culturally responsive to students of color aware of their pedagogical practices and expectations. He noted that many times he often had to address discipline inequities to ensure that African American students were treated fairly. In interacting with teachers, he noted that they resented his authority and often dismissed his suggestions. He believed that teachers were even more resentful when he played an advocate role for the students of color as he noted:

> It took a while to turn it around here. As an administrator it was very difficult [for European American teachers] to accept taking directions or be supervised by a Black person. The truth is the teachers and I had a lot of problems. Whenever any thing happened, they looked at the Black child and not the White child. We would have staff meetings and I would try to get these teachers to change. So there was this big difference here. But I think it took a person who wasn't afraid to confront those issues. By being Black, I certainly had my share with those incidents and needed to communicate that to staff.

At the secondary level, teachers perceived these leaders as "tokens" with little authority. Participants cited conflicting demands of dealing with faculty who saw them only in a certain role and based their perceptions on their own stereotypes. Like Mr. Green, they noted their struggles with teachers, but often felt powerless in getting teachers to change As Mr. Main noted,

> By the third year, the staff finally warmed up to me. In dealing with the faculty, I have had positive ones. I have had some negative ones as well. The unfortunate thing there is not much I can do to change the [European American] teachers' minds.

Two of the secondary participants noted their power struggles of dealing with their administrative peers. They found that often their leadership was questioned when they went beyond their expertise on racial matters. Although in a power position, they were concerned that much of their energies were being spent having to validate their place and competency in these schools. Given their leadership role, they often faced situations where their authority was questioned because of their color. In most cases, these principals struggled with power differences because of always being questioned about who they are and what they represent. As noted by Mr. Winter,

> I knew our principal didn't truly respect me for who I was. I think he was happy that I was there. I cut down on the confusion and keep the Black students in line. But I don't think he respected me. I think after they watched me for a while they respected me. That doesn't mean that we're going over to each other's houses to eat. They have had little exposure to people like me. They don't know how to act and the condescending statements like, "You're very articulate."

Leadership Behavior

Leadership and the influence it has on how organizational and identity groups interact is critical to understanding intergroup conflict. Culturally based stereotypes and expectations of majority followers may influence how they interact with minorities in leadership positions. Therefore, the problem leaders of color have is that they may have values, attitudes, traits, and behaviors that are contrary to traditional beliefs held by the majority group (Chemers & Murphy, 1995). These principals used their leadership as a way to confront intergroup conflicts between themselves and other school participants. This could be understood by (a) their ability to develop a color-conscious leadership style that recognized cultural differences among school participants and (b) their willingness to address racial undertones.

These African American administrators used a "color-conscious" leadership style that recognized cultural differences among various school participants. The assistant principals demonstrated this leadership style when addressing racial issues to ensure that all school participants were treated equitably. Findings from this study suggested these African American leaders were not "color-blind" (see Lewis, 2001) because their race determined how they would lead and be perceived by their diverse group of followers.

These principals used a color-conscious leadership style. Therefore, they were able to address intercultural contact among groups and understood how to navigate between the two cultures without losing their identity. These leaders developed an intercultural relationship with both the identity and dominant group that produced an adaptation of their leadership to respond all the school participants' needs. These African American leaders were able to rotate among the cultural identities of the school participants. Thus they had an understanding of within-group as well as between-group processes.

All of the participants noted that in leading their school participants, it became apparent that they had to incorporate the connections and interrelations among the various groups. Therefore with each group of school participants, whether it was teachers, parents, or students, these administrators soon developed a "color-conscious" leadership style. These participants stated that parts of their roles were to understand the meaning and implications of being an outsider, yet behaviorally they had to be flexible to lead their traditional organizations. Developing a color-conscious ability was important for them to remain in these settings. As noted,

> Everything that occurs at this school is racial. It's simply situational. But if you deal with it as racial you need to point out things. Those kinds of things have to happen. As a leader, I learned all of the fears and concerns that teachers have about these kids and how that affects my decisions. Don't have people wondering what you are saying and speak like an intellect. That is the language they understand here. In this environment, you have to be a leader who can interact with all the differences.

Each assistant principal, in different ways, described the significance of his or her relationship with European American and African American students. These principals expressed that although their exchanges and responses varied as they interacted with various group-level cultures, they were all equally important. For the European American students, it was more about dispelling stereotypes in their interactions with this group. In leading a homogeneous school, many noted the need to assert their authority so they would be perceived as competent.

Because of their group-level racial understandings, they believed their leadership with African American students took on another level of interaction. In leading African American students, these administrators noted that they wore many hats for these students. Their leadership focused on being "mom," strengthening these students' identity, and serving as a racial advocate. Although in many ways these participants addressed their concerns of needing to be fair in their leadership practices, they felt the tensions of having to balance how other school participants perceived them. They were strong in their commitment and were willing to make additional efforts for students. As Ms. Boyd explained,

Being a Black administrator in an all White environment with a few Black kids. It's like being a mom where you don't have a role. Sometimes my Black kids will come in and I will tell them which hat am I wearing? I tell them they have to wear a belt and they can't wear their pants like that. Then one will come in and they are crying, I say do I need my "girlfriend hat" on today?

Due to their color-conscious leadership, these principals made concerted efforts to hold teachers accountable for the "deseg" students at their schools. In particular, these participants noted the conflicting relationships they had when they interacted with teachers about the students of color. These relationships were strained by how these leaders pushed a leadership style that forced teachers to examine their own "color-blind" approaches with students. In general the participants noted that they often pressed the European American teachers to hold high expectations and to treat the African American students fairly. As noted,

I think leadership to [European American] teachers is dependent on how they deal with children and the expectations they hold for them. If you have a sense of equity in the classroom, then everyone should be responsible. Teachers' body language tells a lot to the students here. And if there is a situation, I will not hesitate to bring it to the teachers' attention. I have high standards and am pretty vocal about things.

Conclusion

This study examined the important role leaders of color play in leading and managing sources of conflict that occur in suburban desegregated schools. This study revealed there were multiple sources of intergroup conflict that influenced their leadership decisions. For this study, there were incompatible goals among the school groups that resulted in-group boundaries and cultural differences among the school participants. Due to these group boundaries, the assistant principals struggled with power differences and what that meant in leading and facilitating intercultural contact among identity and organizational groups.

For organizations to be effective, all leaders must understand how organizational groups and identity groups relate to each other. The African American administrators in this study had an understanding of how to address the two-way nature of intercultural contact among groups and understood how to rotate back and forth among the identity groups of their school participants. Leaders of color face multiple challenges in how majority followers will respond to their authority. They have to understand the cultural variations among groups of followers and how that will influence their effectiveness.

Further research needs to be conducted to examine how principals of color negotiate boundaries of race in suburban contexts. Much could be learned about their color-conscious approach to ensure equitable practices for all schoolchildren. Few studies have examined leaders of color in suburban contexts; therefore, the emergence of leadership influence structures on intergroup conflict among minority and majority school participants and the role of race and ethnicity in this process needs additional investigation.

Clearly, the research presented would cause one to carefully examine the assumption that leaders of color play an important role in creating an inclusive school for all students. By promoting a "color-conscious" leadership in these contexts, these African American administrators may provide insights on what skills are needed to understand within-group as well as between-group processes. As noted in the findings, these leaders were able to rotate among the cultural identities and incorporate the connections and interrelationships among the groups.

Although this was an exploratory study, findings from this research might have implications for preparing principals in how to respond to intergroup conflict. According to Chen and Van Velsor (1996) bicultural identity of people of color is often an undervalued strength within the organization. Having a bicultural identity may enable leaders to move back and forth between cultural expectations and norms of two or more cultures. Therefore, leaders become cultural integrators and facilitators in creating common ground among groups.

Emerging literature on global leadership implies that leaders can no longer focus on task and organizational goals only (Chen & Van Velsor, 1996). In motivating a diverse group of followers, leaders must create a one-on-one leader–member relationship where they must create and facilitate new meaning out of diverse viewpoints. Therefore, we need to identify leaders who can tolerate ambiguity among the group identities, develop inclusive skills, develop cultural sensitivity, and have a global mind-set.

Given that our schools are demographically changing, findings from this study about these African American leaders who had a "color-conscious" leadership that allowed them to move back and forth between groups are timely. These leaders appeared to have a broad view so they were able to handle intergroup tensions and facilitate new boundaries in finding common ground among the participants. Thus, they were behaviorally flexible to enhance these school participants' awareness about responding to the African American students.

Although these principals often struggled with their followers' image management, they were able to develop an open-minded learning orientation despite these perceptions. Findings revealed that these administrators were able to move from their own cultural group to work with these school participants. Consequently, their followers benefited, as these administrators were responsible for dispelling stereotypes and proved they were competent leaders. As African American leaders, they developed the capacity to be open-minded, continuous learners, relationship builders, and people developers.

These "color-conscious" leaders were cultural integrators and consensus builders who had acquired a great deal of understanding about diversity of groups and were able to establish leader–member trust. Whether due to their ethnic backgrounds or leadership capabilities, these skills are critical in leading heterogeneous groups in responding to the needs of all students.

The findings suggest that principals in suburban or desegregated contexts play an important role in responding to intergroup conflict that occurs between students of color and European American school participants. Principals must examine their leadership in how they respond to issues of diversity and react to intergroup conflicts. Leadership in managing issues of diversity requires that the principals create trust, establish teams that dispel stereotypical roles for students of color, and promote dialogue on pedagogical differences in responding to the learning needs of students of color.

References

Alderfer, C. P. (1977). Group and intergroup relations. In J. R. Hackman & J. L. Suttle (Eds.), *Improving life at work* (pp. 277–296). Santa Monica, CA: Goodyear.

Alderfer, C. P., Alderfer, C. J., Tucker, L., & Tucker, R. (1980). Diagnosing race relations in management. *Journal of Applied Psychology, 16,* 135–166.

Alderfer, C. P., & Smith, K. K. (1982). Studying intergroup relations embedded in organizations. *Administration Science Quarterly, 27,* 36–65.

Andersen, M. L. (1993). Studying across difference: Race, class, and gender in qualitative research. In J. H. Stanfield, II & R. M. Dennis (Eds.), *Race and ethnicity in research methods* (pp. 39–52). Newbury Park, CA: Sage.

Ayman, R. (1993). Leadership perceptions: The role of gender and culture. In M. Chemers & R. Ayman (Eds.), *Leadership theory and research: Perspectives and directions* (pp. 137–166). San Diego, CA: Academic.

Boyatzis, R. (1998). *Transforming qualitative information: Thematic analysis and code development.* Thousand Oaks, CA: Sage.

Chemers, M. (1993). An integrative theory of leadership. In M. Chemers & R. Ayman (Eds.), *Leadership theory and research: Perspectives and directions* (pp. 239–319). San Diego, CA: Academic.

Chemers, M. M., & Murphy, S. E. (1995). Leadership and diversity in groups and organizations. In M. M. Chemers, S. Oskamp, & M. A. Costanzo (Eds.), *Diversity in organizations: New perspectives for a changing workplace* (pp. 157–190). Thousand Oaks, CA: Sage.

Chen, C., & Van Velsor, E. (1996). New directions for research and practice in diversity leadership. *Leadership Quarterly, 7,* 285–302.

Conrad, C. (1982). Grounded theory: An alternative approach in higher education. *The Review of Higher Education, 5,* 259–269.

Cox, T. (1994). *Cultural diversity in organizations: Theory, research, and practice.* San Francisco: Berrett-Koehler.

Greenhaus, J., Parasuraman, S., & Wormley, W. (1990). Effects of race on organizational experiences, job performance evaluations, and career outcomes. *Academy of Management Journal, 23,* 665–683.

Lewis, A. (2001). There is no "race" in the schoolyard: Color-blind ideology in an (almost) all-white school. *American Educational Research Association, 38,* 781–811.

Merriam, S. (1988). *Case study research in education: A qualitative approach.* San Francisco: Jossey-Bass.

Nkomo, S., & Cox, T. (1996). Diverse identities in organizations. In S. Clegg, C. Hardy, & W. Nords (Eds.), *Handbook of organization studies* (pp. 338–356). Thousand Oaks, CA: Sage.

Ragins, B. R. (1995). Diversity, power, and mentorship in organizations: A cultural, structural, and behavioral perspective. In M. M. Chemers, S. Oskamp, & M. A. Costanzo (Eds.), *Diversity in organizations: New perspectives for a changing workplace* (pp. 91–132). Thousand Oaks, CA: Sage.

Stanfield, J. H., II. (1993). Epistemological considerations. In J. H. Stanfield, II & D. M. Routledge (Eds.), *Race and ethnicity in research methods* (pp. 16–39). Newbury Park, CA: Sage.

Teachers' Perceptions of Intergroup Conflict in Urban Schools

Stella C. Bell
Texas A & M University

The purpose of this article is to examine how teachers of color and European American teachers perceive intergroup conflict in urban schools. This research studies the various types of intergroup conflict that occur between teachers of color and European American teachers in urban schools and how it affects their working relationship. The properties of intergroup conflict identified in this study were areas that caused tensions between majority and minority groups. These conflicts occurred when these groups had opposing interests, and it became problematic in how they responded to students of color.

Urban public schools are changing to serve an increasingly diverse student population. As the number of students of color increases and the teaching workforce continues to be dominated by European American teachers, with fewer numbers of teachers of color, it is crucial to understand how these groups of teachers interact and respond to each other. When European American teachers and teachers of color interact, certain conditions will influence how they work collaboratively in these contexts (Alderfer & Smith, 1982; Alderfer, Tucker, & Tucker, 1980; Cox, 1994). This article examines how teachers of color and European American teachers perceive intergroup conflict in urban schools. This research studies the various types of intergroup conflict that occur between teachers of color

Requests for reprints should be sent to Stella C. Bell, Texas A & M University, College Station, TX 77843. E-mail: bellstella@aol.com and European American teachers in urban schools and how it affects their working relationship.

Theoretical Framework

Embedded Intergroup Theory

As a way to understand group and cultural identities with both teachers of color and European American teachers in urban schools, the researcher used embedded intergroup theory to code and analyze the data. This theoretical framework was useful in describing the types of intergroup conflict that occur among groups of teachers in urban schools. When conflicts occur within diverse groups, it is either directly or indirectly related to cultural group identities. Therefore, the theoretical framework of embedded intergroup theory offers an understanding of the sources of conflict that occur in schools due to issues of diversity (Nkomo & Cox, 1996).

According to Alderfer (1982), many organizations consisted of two types of groups: identity groups and organization groups. Identity group members are those that share common biological characteristics, participate in equivalent historical experiences, and hold similar worldviews. An organizational group is one in which members share common organizational positions, participate in common work experiences, and have similar organizational views (Alderfer, 1982; Nkomo & Cox, 1996). According to embedded intergroup theory, individuals and organizations constantly attempt to manage potential conflicts arising from the interactions between identity groups and the organizational group (Nkomo & Cox, 1996). Research on intergroup differences examines the impact of minority workers in majority organizations.

Cox's (1994) research on group identities provides a broad overview to examine how workers define themselves, as well as how other groups view their differences. The significance of intergroup theory for understanding individual identity helps conceptualize the effects of diverse identities within a larger organizational context (Nkomo & Cox, 1996). Embedded intergroup theory argues that individuals often feel a connection to their identity group. Thus, people in organizations are a function of their identity and not always their organization group membership.

Properties of Intergroup Conflict

The presence of cultural diversity offers a number of potential benefits for organizations. Such diversity also presents certain difficulties that must be given attention in the management of diverse workgroups (Cox, 1994). Rummel (1976) stated that intergroup conflict has two distinguishing features: (a) group boundaries and group characteristics that contribute to differences and (b) how conflict is directly or indirectly related to cultural group identities. Therefore, in working with various ethnically different groups, one must understand how group boundaries and cultural differences affect one's cultural group identity. Cox (1994) contended that group identities are an integral part of the individual's personality. Therefore, much of what is commonly referred to as personality clash may actually be a manifestation of group identity-related conflict.

In the context of cultural diversity in organizations, intergroup conflict occurs between the majority group and the various minority groups represented, as well as among the minority groups themselves. Various researchers have identified multiple sources of conflict and refer to how one condition of discord seems to affect another (Alderfer, 1982; Alderfer et al., 1980; Cox, 1994). Furthermore, in the context of intergroup conflict, these conditions will influence how the leader and majority and minority groups will react to each other (Cox, 1994). The nine properties of intergroup conflict are (a) competing goals, (b) competition for resources, (c) cultural differences, (d) power differences, (e) conformity versus identity affirmation, (f) group boundaries, (g) affective patterns, (h) cognitive formations, and (i) leadership behavior (Figure 1).

The theoretical framework of embedded intergroup and properties of intergroup conflict theories are useful in describing the problems that may occur between teachers of color and European American teachers in how they respond to their diverse student population. When European American teachers and teachers of color interact, certain conditions will influence how they work collaboratively in these contexts (Alderfer & Smith, 1982; Alderfer et al., 1980; Cox, 1994). Therefore, this theory may provide more insights on the cultural incongruities that may occur among various groups of ethnically diverse teachers in these contexts.

Competing Goals: Differences among majority and nonmajority workers in competing goals that are influenced by norms, goal priorities, and work styles among and between these groups (Cox, 1994).

Competition for Resources: Allocation of resources that are influenced by embedded organizational issues such as acknowledgment of group identities in regulating jobs, training priorities, and expansion of resources (Cox, 1994).

Cultural Differences: Cultural differences between group members of different groups occur due to misunderstandings and misperceptions (Cox, 1994).

Power Differences: Majority groups hold advantages over minority groups in the power structure of the organization. Intergroup hostility between groups results in disagreements over the redistribution of power. Minority group density in organizations poses a threat to the existing power structure and provides an opportunity for those who are powerless. The types of resources that can be obtained and used differ among groups. Power differences among groups influence the group's boundaries between the majority and nonmajority workers (Alderfer, 1982; Cox, 1994).

Conformity versus Identity Affirmation: The tension between majority and minority group members over the preservation of minority group identity (Cox, 1994).

Group Boundaries: Both physical and psychological group boundaries determine group membership. Transactions among groups are regulated by variations in the permeability of the boundaries (Alderfer, 1982).

Affective Patterns: The severity of intergroup conflict relates to the polarized feelings among the groups. Group members split their feelings so that positive feelings are associated with their group and negative feelings are associated with other groups (Alderfer, 1982).

Cognitive Formations: Due to group boundaries, power differences, and affective patterns, group members develop their own language, influence members' perceptions of subjective and objective criteria of other groups and work efforts, and transmit propositions about other groups in relation to their own group members (Alderfer, 1982).

Leadership Behavior: The group leader and other group representatives reflect the boundaries of groups and how they will interact. Members of a similar group reflect power differences, affective patterns, and cognitive formations of their group in relation to the other group. The role of the leader in a network of intergroup relations determines the intensification of intergroup conflict (Alderfer, 1977, 1982).

Figure 1. Properties of Intergroup Conflict

Methodology

Data Collection

This was a qualitative study that used a case study approach (Merriam, 1988) to examine the perceptions that teachers of color and European American teachers had of intergroup conflict in urban contexts. The researcher contacted an urban school district in the south regarding their willingness to participate in the project. The researcher then identified schools and principals with diverse teaching staffs to select participants for this study. As a way to make the initial contact, the researcher personally visited with the teachers of color and the European American teachers. This first contact with these groups of teachers was used to focus the inquiry at the single-case level of analysis (Merriam, 1988). Additional secondary interviews were conducted to further investigate teachers' concerns regarding intergroup conflict. The questions for the interviews were developed based on the properties of intergroup conflict. All of the interviews with teachers of color and European American teachers were taped and later transcribed for recurring themes.

Of the 20 participants, there were 3 African American teachers and 7 Hispanic participants (teachers of color) and 10 European American teachers (Table 1). All of the teachers who were interviewed were at the elementary level. The researcher excluded counselors, special education teachers, and parents from the pool of participants because of the different type of subject matter and interactions within the group. The researcher analyzed the African American and Hispanic teachers' data collectively and did not separate these into ethnic groups. The rationale for this decision was due to the small sample of both Hispanic and African American teachers. Further studies may need to be undertaken to examine conflicts that may occur among ethnic groups of teachers.

Data Sources

District and Schools

The study took place in an urban desegregated school district in the South. The majority of the district's student population was African American and Hispanic (students of color). The total number of minorities in the district was 61%, with 42% identified as "at-risk" students. Thirty-eight percent of the teachers within the district had 5 or fewer years of teaching experience. The district teacher turnover rate was at least 16% for the year. The district's professional teaching staff consisted of 29% teachers of color and 71% European American teachers.

The two schools at which these participants were interviewed were selected because they were led by African American principals, and the schools' demographics reflected the district. The student demographic for School A was approximately 51% students of color and 49% European Americans. The student population for School B was one third African American, one third Hispanic, and one third European American students.

Table 1

Data Sources of Participants

ID Number	Ethnicity	Gender	Years of Experience	Teaching Assignment	Out of District
649	AA	F	8	P	No
221	H	F	11	I	No
814	H	F	1	P	No
231	H	F	1	P	No
454	H	F	2	1	Yes
555	H	F	2	P	No
153	H	F	10	P	No
929	AA	F	28	P	No
123	H	F	1	P	No
711	AA	F	5	1	No
325	EA	F	18	1	Yes
466	EA	F	10	1	Yes
351	EA	F	2	P	Yes
114	EA	F	16	P	No
815	EA	F	17	P	No
439	EA	F	1	P	No
462	EA	F	7	1	Yes
489	EA	F	1	P	No
444	EA	M	3	P	No
141	EA	F	5	P	No
876	AA	F	22	1	Yes
127	AA	M	5	1	Yes

Note. AA = African American; H = Hispanic; EA = European American; P = Primary; I = Intermediate.

Principal A had been employed by the school district for 20 years in various capacities from classroom teacher and instructional coordinator to the principal. Principal B had only 5 years of experience in the district as a teacher or coach in the middle and elementary schools. This was his first appointment as a principal. Both Principals A and B felt that there were tensions in their respective building among these groups of teachers.

Selection of Teacher Participants

For this study, the criteria for selecting these participants was based on these teachers' experiences, ethnicity, teacher leadership abilities, and academic success with students of color. Also, the 20 teachers were selected because they were recognized as being sensitive to culturally diverse issues

Teachers' Perceptions of Intergroup Conflict

and were considered collaborative team builders. Of the 10 teachers of color, all were women, 3 were African American, and 7 were Hispanic. Of the 10 European American teachers, 9 were women and 1 was a man. This pool of applicants allowed the researcher to identify a cross-section of teachers' perceptions about intergroup conflict (Guba, 1993; see Table 1).

Teachers of Color

Three African American female teachers were interviewed for this study. The African American teachers' professional experiences ranged from 5 to 28 years. The African American teachers' average years at the same school was 5 years. The African American teacher with the most experience had graduated from a historically Black college in the state. However, the other 2 African American teachers had attended other universities. The African American teachers had a total of 11 years of experience. Furthermore, all 3 African American teachers were educated outside their district of employment. Each African American teacher's personal experiences brought uniqueness to the urban school. One African American teacher grew up in a predominantly European American environment, whereas the other 2 grew up in an integrated neighborhood and a predominantly African American neighborhood (see Table 1).

Seven Hispanic teachers were interviewed for this study. Four of the Hispanic teachers were born and grew up in border towns near Mexico. However, the other 3 Hispanic teachers were from an urban city with personal experiences and lifestyles of middle-class status. Of the 7 Hispanic teachers, 3 of them were the first to receive college degrees in their family. The average number of years of teaching experience for the Hispanic teachers was 9. Six of the Hispanic teachers did not have any out-of-the district experience, whereas 1 Hispanic teacher had taught in another school district. All 7 Hispanic teachers had professional teaching experiences in both bilingual and nonbilingual classrooms. Six Hispanic teachers were primary teachers versus 1 Hispanic, who was an intermediate teacher. Five of the Hispanic teachers spoke Spanish and communicated fluently in their native language; 2 Hispanic teachers were English dominant.

European American Teachers

Ten European American teachers participated in the study. Nine of the European American teachers were women and one was a male teacher. The average professional teaching experience for the European American teachers was 8 years. Their experiences ranged from 1 to 18 years. Seven of the teachers taught primary grades, whereas 3 European American teachers taught intermediate grades. All the European American teachers were hired to teach in predominately low socioeconomic schools in the district. However, only 1 European American teacher had experience in and was from outside the district. Nine of the European American teachers grew up in middle-class neighborhoods, whereas 1 teacher noted that she had been raised in an affluent background. This European American teacher's lifestyle was so different that she noted the adjustment she had to make in responding to the students of color. Two European American teachers had completed their student teaching experiences in their respective schools.

Data Analysis

The researcher used a qualitative thematic strategy to categorize and interpret the data. This methodological process led to a single-case level of analysis from which data were aggregated to incorporate a thematic approach. This analytical procedure allowed important themes and categories to emerge inductively from the data across cases (Miles & Huberman, 1984). Findings from the interviews were clustered by key themes across schools and single cases. The researcher used the prior research-driven approach to identify themes and to develop a coding process (Boyatzis, 1998). In establishing the reliability for this study, the data were analyzed using what Conrad (1982) called a constant comparative method. This coding process was constructed by comparing data from this study with intergroup theory (Alderfer, 1982; Cox, 1994) and properties of intergroup conflict (Cox, 1994; see Table 1).

As a way to bring about a collective interpretation in the data analysis, the researcher believed it was important to understand the complexities in collecting and analyzing cross-cultural research. Stanfield and Dennis (1993) asserted that in race and ethnicity research, comparative analysis can be interpreted in a number of ways. They believe that researchers in mainstream disciplines rarely reflect on the effects of their own racial identities and how that influences their interpretations. There is also the norm in social sciences to assume that European American realities can be generalized to people of color. Stanfield and Dennis further argued that there are ethical considerations in researching people of color because of cultural, class, and gender differences, and a special sensitivity is required to study these discrepancies.

The researcher completed the interviews with both teachers of color and European American participants. However, the analysis was a collaborative endeavor between the African American researcher and a female European American colleague. In this cross-cultural analysis, both researchers analyzed the data separately to ensure a reliable coding system. Once the data were examined, the researcher addressed different interpretations to ensure interrater reliability and to establish a fair analysis of the perceptions of intergroup conflict reported by teachers of color and European American teachers. Discussions about the differences in the cross-cultural interpretation of the data between the two researchers were established to ensure a reliable and trustworthy interpretation of the findings (Merriam, 1988). There was a consistency of judgment between the researchers to determine the judgment on code development and coding (Boyatzis, 1998).

This study was conceived as an exploratory investigation to examine how teachers of color and European American teachers perceive intergroup conflict and its impact on their exchanges in urban schools. Given the restricted focus of this study, the researcher identified a number of possible limitations. Although the pool of participants was small and may only be generalized to urban schools, the participants' experiences and perceptions provided much commonality in terms of themes and findings. The participants were from a variety of personal and educational experiences, backgrounds, and gender differences, and their cultural identity may or may not have influenced their understanding of intergroup conflict. The scope of the study was limited to two elementary schools in an urban district and was not representative of all schools in general. Finally, the researcher's personal and professional experiences and background knowledge revealed divergent constructions of reality about the context of the study. However, given these limitations, the researcher believes these teachers' perceptions of intergroup conflict were valid and genuine.

Findings

Findings from this study revealed that intergroup conflict occurred between the teachers of color and the European American teachers. Based on the properties of intergroup conflict, three major themes emerged from the data. These were incompatible goals, group boundaries, and power differences. Both the teachers of color and the European American teachers identified similar intergroup conflicts, but perceived them differently. Although both groups of teachers noted incompatible goals, differences between the teachers of color and European American teachers were in how European American teachers perceived their own interest versus the collective importance of racial affiliation by the teachers of color. Group boundaries for the European American teachers occurred due to the strong alliance that was formed among teachers of color. European American teachers expressed discomfort with group boundaries, because they were uneasy in their communications with the teachers and students of color. Power differences were reflected in how the European American teachers were color-blind to the needs of students of color and were unwilling to change their instructional practices. Thus, the ensuing discussion reflects these groups of teachers' perceptions of intergroup conflict and the impact it had on their ability to respond to the needs of students of color (Figure 2).

Incompatible Goals

One area of intergroup conflict is incompatible goals that occur between minority and majority workers. Thus, how people interact and respond to others may be influenced by their differences in norms and work styles (Cox, 1994). That is, how people interact and respond to others that are different from them are influenced by norms, goal priorities, and work styles among these groups (Cox, 1994). The first theme that emerged from this study was incompatible goals, which occurred among the teachers of color and European American teachers. In this study, the incompatible goals became apparent in the following ways: (a) Teachers of color noted strong racial connections in meeting the educational needs of students of color, whereas the European American teachers viewed their desires as a priority; and (b) teachers' perceptions of their roles differed, as teachers of color viewed themselves as cultural translators and role models. Consequently, the European American counterparts perceived themselves as authority figures in maintaining classroom control.

Incompatible goals
  1. Racial connection versus self
  2. Cultural translators versus classroom managers
Group boundaries
  1. Strong cultural alliance
  2. Communication and cultural differences
Power differences
  1. Color blindness and promotion of traditional pedagogy
  2. Shared culture and racial affiliation

Figure 2. Properties of Intergroup Conflict: Emergent Themes, Teachers of Color, and European American Teachers

Racial connection versus self. Incompatible goals between these two groups of teachers were apparent in serving the needs of students of color. The teachers of color had a strong cultural background to their group identity that made them aware of the need to ensure a strong sense of their own racial identity and to become advocates for their students. Due to this cultural connection, teachers of color developed a strong collective group membership. Due to this membership, these teachers were conscious of the importance of maintaining high expectations for themselves and their students of color. The teachers of color articulated their interpretations for high expectations from their past experiences and the community's desire for people of color to succeed in life. A teacher of color noted,

> I think it is a good working relationship. I have not had any problems in my years of teaching. I seem to get along with my peers. Because it is about one purpose and that is children and learning. I mean, it is a job you do but you learn how to work with all ethnic and nationalities of teachers. I think, in a way, I have higher goals and high expectations for children of color. I push them. Sometimes, I might push them too hard. But, that is just the way I feel that I am supposed to do. I want children to do the best that they can. It is my job to do that. I had good role models. I had excellent role models inside and outside the family. And I think I have high expectations for "myself" and children of color particularly.

Because there were few teachers of color at these schools, both the African American and Hispanic teachers stated how important their racial identities were to them. Whether it was their skin color, language, or relationship bonding to other people of color, these teachers of color noted the need to retain a sense of their cultural identity. The teachers of color felt that they needed to talk with other people of color without being conscious about their actions. The goals of teachers of color for needing to affirm their cultural identity created a continuous internal struggle of either acting too ethnic or not ethnic enough. As one of these teachers of color noted,

> Even in the makeup of my Anglo teacher friends, I don't feel comfortable with making jokes the way I do with my Hispanic friends. I have a close relationship with some of the custodians (Hispanic). I will tease them and say, you know, my room is always clean. Sometimes, I feel comfortable making those kinds of jokes and sometimes I don't. Or I have heard other Anglo teachers say, you know the custodians pretend not to be able to speak English. And there is a part of me that gets offended by comments like that.

> I am very much into bilingual education. Spanish was my first language. I spoke Spanish until I was about four. I am very proud of my background.
>
> As an African American teacher, you always hear "give back to your community." And you get to a point that it is a strong feeling that you have. I don't know why, but I know it is strong and it is real.

Another aspect of incompatible goals with their European American counterparts was that both the Hispanic and African American teachers felt that they were constantly reminded of their racial presence, their language, and physical differences as well. They believed that their European American teachers held certain beliefs about them that resulted in them needing to preserve their own identity. The concerns of the teachers of color about being one of a few teachers of color in the school, while trying to maintain one's racial identity, resulted in intergroup conflicts with the other European American teachers. As these teachers noted,

> It is important to me, that we should be proud of our language and culture. So that other teachers will know that because we are Hispanic, and Spanish is our first language, there is more to us than just that.
>
> I have always pretty much been the only African American or very close to the only African American in a lot of places that I have been. So, I have kinda lived in both worlds. It doesn't bother me as much as I am sure it bothers some people. I am very proud of being Black, no matter where.

In contrast, there were incompatible goals for the European American teachers. Many European American teachers were boastful about getting their school loans deferred. They did not envision themselves as long term in urban schools and only wanted to remain long enough to get their college student loans repaid. The European American teachers' financial gain became their first priority, in contrast to the teachers of color, who viewed their purposes differently. The European American teachers were concerned with serving only 5 years in urban schools and then moving to suburban schools in the area. A teacher noted,

> Well, actually one of the reasons I took this job. Well, I needed a job. I was just out of school. The other thing, I had a kind of loan, and if I worked in a low-income school for 5 years, then each year that I was there then part of my loan would be canceled. And by the end of

5 years, the whole thing was gone. By the end of 5 years, it was paid off. So, I did not have to pay back any of my student loans.

Another aspect of incompatible goals was the way in which the European American teachers focused on their needs and not on their students' concerns. With this self-first perspective, these teachers were more concerned with their time, long working hours, and having no personal life. This was in contrast to teachers of color, who never mentioned these same issues. The European American teachers' lack of acknowledgment about racial matters and limited understanding about their students of color resulted in them only responding to their needs. For instance,

> The other school was very well represented with African American teachers. I would hear little things about tensions between different teachers. I was so busy working 70 hours a week and crying the other hours. Because it was like, is this what I am going to do with my life for the rest of my life as long as I live? This is hard. I know that things existed but I did not know what they were and I am not convinced that it . . .That I am not convinced that it had anything to do with race. I don't know why, but maybe I am silly . . . maybe I just don't get it.

Cultural translators versus classroom managers. There were incompatible goals in how teachers of color and European American teachers believed their students perceived them. As cultural translators, the teachers of color believed they were to be positive role models for children of color. To the teachers of color, cultural translators were interpreters who shared and maintained the traditions, heritage, norms, and values of their culture. In addition, as a cultural translator, the teachers of color believed they needed to use instructional practices to reinforce the learning styles of children of color. Teachers of color recognized the importance of cultural translators to share knowledge about ethnic traditions beyond the once or twice a year celebrations. The teachers of color wanted children of color to identify with their heritage in a positive and constructive manner. The teacher noted,

> So, again, I have really lived in both worlds. So it doesn't bother me, but what bothers me about it is I want the children to see more models. More models like me. They [children of color] need to see themselves. They deserve to see themselves in others in a positive and influential position. I feel so strongly that every kid deserves to see at least one

time, someone from their culture as their teacher. I think that is so important.

One Hispanic teacher shared her frustration about having high expectations for children of color and the importance of being a translator of culture. This teacher was very concerned with teaching students about their culture. She believed that the Hispanic culture is a vast and complex society with positive and outstanding contributions to the world. She believed it was her role to share that with her students. The teacher noted,

> We are researching the Hispanic characters. We are researching about Latin American countries. I want them to know that they are Hispanics that can make it and do make a difference to accomplish things in life. So, they will know just because they are Hispanic and Spanish is your first language, it does not mean that you can't make it somewhere. It was important to me, for my team members to teach more than just the basic once or twice celebrations. There is more to us than just that.

In contrast, European American teachers failed to see the importance of engaging in culturally relevant interactions with their students of color. The incompatible goal for European American teachers was to place less emphasis on students' ethnic development and to focus their energies on classroom management. These European American teachers believed that their students would improve their learning if there was an orderly classroom environment. The European American teachers' management strategies were different from the teachers of color. Hence, there were tensions between them and the teachers of color over student discipline issues at these schools. The European American teachers revealed that they did not have the same relationship with the children of color as their colleagues. The European American teacher noted,

> The strange and unusual thing was all they [students of color] did was look up to their African American teachers. They [teachers of color] tended to have more control in their classrooms. You could pass by their classroom and those kids were all sitting in a row. I don't know what they were teaching, but when you walked into some of the other classrooms, they would be very noisy, with lots of activity going on. You know they would be all sitting and doing their work.

Group Boundaries

Group boundaries that occur in the workplace may result in tensions among groups. Group boundaries among diverse groups occur because of misunderstandings and misperceptions that are related to the different worldviews of culture groups. Alderfer and Smith (1982) believed that cultural differences and group boundaries become manifested when majority group members make decisions on what is acceptable and establish the norms and expectations for all to follow. Findings from this study revealed that group boundaries were established due to (a) the strong cultural alliance formed among teachers of color and (b) the problems of the communication differences between the teachers of color and European American teachers.

Strong cultural alliance. Alderfer (1982) indicated that both physical and psychological group boundaries determine group membership. Because there were so few African American and Hispanic teachers, these teachers of color developed a strong cultural connection among themselves. Thus, group boundaries were established with their European American counterparts when they met separately in groups. Again, the teachers of color were set apart from the other European American teachers by their skin, language, or traditions. Thus, these teachers of color visibility created group boundaries with European American teachers because of their alliance in the school.

The teachers of color used their cultural alliance to ensure that the students of color were not exposed to stereotypical views of history, and as cultural translators they supported ethnic traditions throughout the school year. Teachers of color encouraged the celebration for African American Heritage Month and Cinco de Mayo holidays. Furthermore, the teachers of color used culturally relevant pedagogy and brought in formal and informal resource speakers as a way for them to connect with their students of color. Some teachers of color noted,

> At the beginning of the year, we had kids who did not want to know about Mexican American cultures or African American cultures except the people of that particular color. I just think it is important for them to know about it all. It is part of who they are and who their families are. . . . I know that my Hispanic students, especially for some reason when they heard me speak Spanish, it just sort of clicked inside. And they started including all the things from our culture, because they knew that I understood. It opened up something for them. . . . They started writing Spanish words in their writings.

But, I would do things like in our planning time—my contribution would be like a book with characters of color as a positive role model. When we did grandparents' day, I brought a woman from my church who was an 80-year-old woman, African American. I have tried to make a contribution that way without being too explicit.

African American and Hispanic teachers' cultural alliance resulted in them becoming advocates for themselves in how teacher assignments were arranged. Teachers of color noted they were concerned with placing only one African American teacher on a team composed of mostly European American teachers. The teachers of color acknowledged the loneliness in an organization without some kind of team connection. Teachers of color noted that it was a struggle to keep racially connected with other teachers of color, as the school assignments often kept them isolated.

The teachers of color noted that crossing group boundaries was a part of life, which they believed that the European American teachers were hesitant to do. The teachers of color identified group differences and acknowledged the need for compassion by the European American teachers. The contentment of being satisfied in the environment and the skepticism of trying to retain one's self is a myth, as shared in the following quotes from teachers of color:

I hope I am not misjudging how they (European American teachers) really felt. But, they seem to be very loving and caring. Of course, you will have your few [European American teachers] who will not come in with the rest of us. Even when I did not have a partner. You know some grade levels have more difficulty. They don't seem to do well. But, they try. I mean, they put forth the effort. But, when I was ready to go, I was ready. The reassignment meant I would not be in a regular classroom. That caused me to be very concerned for the children of color, you know about positive role models for our children.

I do know that everybody has difficulties in life. We all have our cross to bear, some more than others. But, it does not necessarily mean that because of our color, sometimes, I feel like not everybody helps each other enough. You know, we are not compassionate enough to each other. Everyone is looking out for themselves. This is not necessary.

Communication and cultural differences. In contrast, the European American teachers' group boundaries were in the area of communication and cultural differences. This was apparent in how European American teachers were hesitant to express their concerns to the teachers of color about their student differences. These European American teachers noted they were uncomfortable addressing racial issues with the teachers of color. They stated they were fearful of being perceived as not sensitive on matters of race, so they limited their communication with the other teachers of color. Therefore, group boundaries were established on the basis of teachers' of color and European American teachers' hesitation to talk about racial concerns. One European American teacher noted this as follows:

> I have noticed [it] with another teacher. I don't know if it would be racism, as much as tension. When we are talking about whether we should have bonding with teachers, or students, whether they should be instructed in which classroom. And I think that has been a source of tension off and on between teachers. And I think for a lot of years. We kinda of just brushed it under the rug, so we don't have to talk about it. But I think that is a sticking point, that division, seems to be where the most difference is.

Another group boundary for the European American teachers was when they had to respond to cultural differences with both the teachers and students of color. In these teachers' interviews, they expressed that they had limited experiences and knowledge about the identities of other groups, which were culturally different from them. These European American teachers' uneasiness to talk about cultural differences, except during specific occasions, left them feeling unsure of themselves. European American teachers' ability to feel comfortable with both positive and negative cultural differences caused conflict during the interactions with the teachers of color. As noted by this European American teacher's comment,

> So we worked very hard to include her [teacher of color] so that she did not feel isolated. You know she is always like, I don't know how to explain it to us . . . but why African Americans have to put grease in their hair. So she would talk about how they never seem to have lice, when we have lice checks. Things like that.

Power Differences

Power differences occur when the majority group holds advantages over the minority groups in the power structure of the organization (Alderfer & Smith, 1982). Intergroup hostility exists among groups over disagreement and redistribution of power. Minority group density in organizations poses a threat to the existing power structure and provides an opportunity for those who are powerless (Cox, 1994). Findings from this study revealed that the teachers of color and European American teachers perceived their responses to power differences differently. For the European American teachers viewed power differences in their "color-blind" approach and promotion of a traditional pedagogy. In contrast, the teachers of color believed that their power was having a shared culture and a racial affiliation with their principals.

Color blindness and promotion of traditional pedagogy. Power differences were apparent between the European American teachers and teachers of color over issues of color-blind talk and their hesitation to acknowledge ethnic identities of children of color. These European American teachers noted that they felt there was too much emphasis in their schools on multicultural and ethnic identity. They believed that when questions were raised on these issues, they were perceived as being "color-blind" and insensitive to the needs of students of color. Power differences became evident when the European American teachers were unwilling to promote a race focus in their classrooms. These European American teachers' wavering on recognizing their students' cultural identities and supporting their heritage, traditions, and language created intergroup conflict with the teachers of color, as revealed in the following quotation:

> Well you know I'd try not to see color, I mean color, use it as an issue only if it comes up. To really be honest with you, I was looking at my grouping cards and you are supposed to put a check by the name at the origin of their ethnic origin and then I have never thought about any one of my students in that way.

Furthermore, European American teachers struggled with teachers of color about what the role of cultural translators was in the school. European American teachers believed it was important for children of color to see teachers like them as well. They were unwilling to believe that only teachers of color were able to make a difference in their students' lives. They did not believe that racial affiliation was the only way to connect with students. The teacher noted,

> I had grown up affluent and I am Anglo. It was a school with a lot of low socioeconomic levels around there. There was a lot of transient people—they would rent until they could not afford it, they would rent

until they got kicked out. He (leader of color) felt like that I could not relate to the kids that you know, families that were barely able to make it from month to month. I think that was more of what it was than just a Black or White thing. It probably was more of being affluent than not.

European American teachers noted power differences over their inability to speak Spanish. Many of the European American teachers did not understand nor did they speak Spanish. They noted their aggravations with teachers of color on when to use English versus Spanish in school duties. These European American teachers were frustrated with their inability to understand what the teachers of color were saying among themselves and to the students. In many ways, the European American teachers' power differences were a way to control when teachers of color could speak Spanish. As noted,

I don't feel threatened either, when Hispanics are talking Spanish. You know, I can understand a little bit of it, but I have often wondered if there might be people who are wondering why are they speaking in Spanish, or are they talking about me?

Power differences between European American teachers and teachers of color were apparent in how teachers believed students of color should be taught. European American teachers felt their use of traditional pedagogy was appropriate in working with their students. For them, they had been trained in "stand and deliver" methods of teaching; therefore, other pedagogical methodologies did not seem suitable for them. As noted earlier, the European American teachers were "self" driven in assuring that they were in control of their students' learning. The European American teachers noted,

She [teacher of color] was a second-year teacher. So, I have paired my math class with her math class, so that she could see how I am handling the curriculum.

She had students of color who were very isolated in their classroom. I just decided as soon as we got through with that meeting we would team together. She was very scared because she had the lessons in front of her, but she really did need to see the model of how to teach it. I showed her lots of strategies.

At the other school a lot of the teachers [African Americans] were not current. They got certified years ago and they complained and griped. We had to show them some new instructional strategies.

Shared culture and racial affiliation. In contrast to the European American teachers' power differences, these teachers of color perceived their power in having a shared culture and racial affiliation with their principals of color. The African American and Hispanic teachers believed there was this ongoing power struggle of who should decide how children should be taught at the school. Due to this shared culture and racial affiliation with their principals, teachers of color believed they should have greater control over curriculum decisions. Therefore, teachers of color created power differences over the European American teachers. Due to their racial affiliation with their principals, these teachers derived a strong sense of influence that they had not experienced in other majority schools. These teachers used their cultural alliance in ways they felt could diminish the European American teachers' authority. As these teachers noted,

> I have a shared culture and a shared understanding with my principal. I mean, we just sit and talk and there are so many things that we have in common. You might have with others, but not really. They [European American] do not understand. You know we have a lot in common because we are the same color. She is a very caring and sensitive woman. She provided me with so much of support. She believes in me and trusts my judgment. I support and respect her power as my leader so much.

> I think the one thing that keeps me here, is that the principal has really allowed and trusted me to do what I feel needs to be done for children. This principal has allowed me to really do my best at whatever it is. We have developed this friendship and camaraderie that you know. She knows my expectations and I know hers. Because I know that as a principal she has certain things that need to be met. She trusts me, and she knows that I am willing to do whatever it takes to get the job done for kids.

Implications

This study examined how teachers of color and European American teachers perceived intergroup conflict in urban schools. The study revealed there were multiple sources of intergroup conflict, which resulted in creating a negative relationship between diverse groups of teachers. Based on the findings, it was apparent that the teachers of color and European American teachers struggled with how to address intergroup conflict. Due to the incompatible goals of how to teach students of color, teachers in these urban contexts could not agree on the importance of racial affiliation and what that means instructionally. Group boundaries were created due to European American teachers' reliance on traditional instructional patterns and the hesitation by teachers of color to address their colleagues practices. Finally, power differences over who had authority over curriculum and student placement decisions became apparent when teachers of color noted their racial affiliation with their principals and shared culture with other teachers of color.

The complexity of intergroup conflict establishes negative relationships among ethnically diverse teachers that have implications for children in urban schools. One approach in dealing with intergroup conflict is to develop a framework to analyze the organizational culture and its impact on teacher relations (Ragins, 1995). Teachers in diverse schools have the chance to determine which groups influence the power structure in these contexts. They also have the ability and the power to create a self-perpetuating cycle that may reinforce inequities on how students of color are treated in these environments. These inequitable power structures between teachers of color and European American teachers must be addressed in managing intergroup conflict that occurs in urban schools.

Based on the findings from this study, I suggest how groups of ethnically diverse teachers can respond to intergroup conflict within an urban school. Teachers who find themselves interacting in diverse groups who may be different due to their gender or ethnic background must consider the cultural experiences of others. A variety of issues are important in creating an inclusive school: (a) different motivational needs and cultural values that may influence other teachers' decisions, (b) communication practices that may affect how other teachers are perceived, and (c) principals' expectations of who is empowered in school decisions.

Open communication practices among diverse groups of teachers are important. The ability to include all voices within the organization provides a clear understanding and interaction. Open communication allows for clarity of cultures and resolution of differences. Teachers must be sensitive to a variety of cultures when they exist, and they must find ways to reduce the negative impact of intergroup conflict. Teachers of color may resolve their responses to intergroup conflict through the understanding of being cultural translators for both European American teachers and students of color.

Teachers are also critical in dealing with structural influences within the organization that can affect intergroup conflict. Concerns over organizational structures (teaming, mentoring, and technical support) often prevent teachers of color from actively participating in school issues.

European American teachers may determine the dominant perceptions for teacher assignments and low expectations for students' performances and may prevent a cultural connection. However, in dealing with intergroup conflict, the European American teachers need to use their positions of influence to equalize group boundaries and power differences between themselves and the teachers of color. However, in leading discussions on how to improve the intergroup perceptions, these groups of teachers may be hesitant to hold each other accountable and responsible for the students of color. Instead, teachers of color become the cultural translators, and European American teachers are left out of the dialogue.

Using a framework to examine behavioral influences within the organizational culture is effective in preventing intergroup conflict (Ragins, 1995). This frame examines the organization and the teachers' interactions to change behaviors, attitudes, and attributions needed to prevent negative group expectations. Problems of the microinequities of majority groups result in the exclusion of informal peer support and networking as a way to support minorities (Ragins, 1995). Ultimately, all teachers play an important role in defining how both groups of teachers are perceived and accepted in school contexts. Findings from this study revealed that intergroup conflict among these groups resulted in mistrust between both the teachers of color and European American teachers.

The findings suggest that leaders in urban schools play an important role in responding to intergroup conflict that occurs between teachers of color and European American teachers. Teachers in this study were unable to create an organizational culture that supported professional opportunities for both groups of teachers. Teachers' intergroup conflict created perceptions that prevented them from establishing a positive rapport with each other. Teachers of color were viewed as cultural translators for students of color, and European American teachers were hesitant to ensure the positive effects of diversity for these students as well. Leaders need to be aware of intergroup conflict among groups of teachers if they are to create an inclusive school.

This study is important because it examines teachers' of color and European American teachers' perceptions regarding intergroup conflicts and identifies the organizational roadblocks that prohibit the establishment of an inclusive school. Teachers must manage the issues of diversity that require them to dispel stereotypes; they must support the use of culturally relevant interactions in responding to the needs of students of color. Finally, teachers of color and European American teachers must respond to intergroup conflict to establish an inclusive school.

References

Alderfer, C. P. (1977). Group and intergroup relations. In J. R. Hackman & J. L. Suttle (Eds.), *Improving life at work* (pp. 227–296). Santa Monica, CA: Goodyear.

Alderfer, C. P. (1982). Problems of changing White males' behaviors and beliefs concerning race relations. In P. S. Goodman & Associates (Eds.), *Change in organizations* (pp. 122–165). San Francisco: Jossey-Bass.

Alderfer, C. P., & Smith, K. K. (1982). Studying intergroup relations embedded in organizations. *Administrative Science Quarterly, 27,* 122–165.

Alderfer, C. P., Tucker, C. J., & Tucker, R. (1980). Diagnosing race relations management. *Journal of Applied Behavioral Science, 16,* 135–166.

Boyatzis, R. E. (1998). *Transforming qualitative information: Thematic analysis and code development.* Thousand Oaks, CA: Sage.

Conrad, C. (1982). Grounded theory: An alternative approach in higher education. *The Review of Higher Education, 5,* 259–269.

Cox, T. H. (1994). *Cultural diversity in organizations: Theory, research and practice.* San Francisco: Berrett-Koehler.

Guba, E. (1993). *The paradigm dialogue.* Newbury Park, CA: Sage.

Merriam, S. B. (1988). *Case study research in education: A qualitative approach.* San Francisco: Jossey-Bass.

Miles, M. B., & Huberman, M. (1984). *Qualitative data analysis: A sourcebook of new methods.* Beverly Hills, CA: Sage.

Nkomo, S., & Cox, T. (1996). Diverse identities in organizations. In S. Clegg, C. Hardy, & W. Nords (Eds.), *Handbook of organization studies* (pp. 338–356). Thousand Oaks, CA: Sage.

Ragins, B. R. (1995). Diversity, power, and membership in organizations. In M. Chemers, M. Costanzo, & S. Oskamp (Eds.), *Diversity in organizations: New perspectives for a changing workplace* (pp. 91–132). Thousand Oaks, CA: Sage.

Rummell, R. J. (1976). *Understanding conflict and war.* New York: Wiley.

Stanfield, J. H., & Dennis, R. (1993). *Race and ethnicity in research methods.* Thousand Oaks, CA: Sage.

Urban School Leaders and the Implementation of Zero-Tolerance Policies: An Examination of Its Implications

Christopher Dunbar, Jr., and Francisco A. Villarruel
Michigan State University

This article examines the responses of school principals from an urban school district to Michigan's zero-tolerance policy. We specifically seek to understand how school leaders interpret and implement the policy and how their administrative discussions subsequently affect the educational experience of children in urban schools. Given that a disproportionately high number of African American and Latino students are negatively affected by this policy, how do school leaders in predominantly African American districts implement it? The findings in this study reveal that the disparate interpretation of the zero-tolerance policy among school leaders and its implementation negatively affects the educational experience of urban students.

The authors thank Harry Matrone and Joyce Piert, doctoral students in Educational Administration at Michigan State University, for their assistance with the data collection. The study was funded in part by the Educational Policy at Michigan State University.

Requests for reprints should be sent to Christopher Dunbar, Jr., Department of Educational Administration, 407 Erickson Hall, Michigan State University, East Lansing, MI 48824.

On January 1, 1995, a new zero-tolerance law took effect in Michigan public schools mandating the permanent expulsion of any student who brought a dangerous weapon to school. This law was implemented in response to heightened fears expressed by the public, which called for stronger preventive measures to address school safety in light of the tragedies that had swept some of our nation's schools. The law originally drafted by Congress focused on truly dangerous and criminal behavior by a student(s), such as gun possession on school property. However, many states, including Michigan, extended these laws to include other weapons such as daggers, dirks, stilettos, knives with blades over 3 in., pocketknives opened by a mechanical device, iron bars, or brass knuckles (Advancement Project/Civil Rights Project, 2000). In addition, zero-tolerance policies have been extended to more types of punishable behaviors, which have ranged from possession of drugs, including Midol and aspirin, to possession of toy guns, insubordination, and disruption (Ayers, Dohrn, & Ayers, 2001), many of which pose little or no threat to school safety.

This article examines the responses of school principals from an urban district to Michigan's zero-tolerance policy. We specifically seek to understand how school leaders interpret and implement the policy and how their practices affect the educational experience of children in their schools. Given that a disproportionately high number of African American and Latino students (Advancement Project/Civil Rights Project, 2000) are negatively affected by this policy, how do school leaders in a predominantly African American district implement the policy? Unlike our earlier work in rural communities, where we discovered that the zero-tolerance policy had minimal impact on the duties of rural school leaders, the findings discussed in this article reveal very different positions on zero-tolerance policies and their implementation by urban school leaders. For example, one urban elementary school administrator responded (when asked for his interpretation of zero tolerance): "Zero tolerance means zero tolerance of weapons, threatening, and bullying. We don't give kids an inch. We don't give them chances!" It is this difference in perspective and its resultant policy implementation that guides this article.

Unfortunately, the consequences of violating zero-tolerance policies vary by district and by violation, but, generally, the harsher the perceived violation, the graver the punishment. School personnel may use discretionary judgment, for example, to suspend students for up to 180 days for vague and questionable violations of policies that move beyond the intent of zero tolerance (Dohrn, 2001; Ladson-Billings, 2001). For more egregious acts, such as weapons violations, schools are required to expel students for up to 180 days—one full academic school year. The law has become a quick solution for a complex set of circumstances. That is, it has become a cure-all, fix-all solution that absolves parents, teachers, and school leaders from an obligation to meet the educational needs of all students.

Although proponents of these policies assert that it removes behaviorally disruptive students from schools, thus making these environments safer, there are a series of unintended consequences that opponents of this policy assert are overly punitive and affect the educational opportunities and developmental pathways for youth (Advancement Project/Civil Rights Project, 2000). Research, for example, has noted that youth who fall behind their age cohorts are more likely to drop out of school or experience failure on their return or to engage in a higher proportion of juvenile acts, eventually ending up in the juvenile justice system (Michie, 2001). Moreover, communities who suspend youth generally do not have alternative schools that can provide educational alternatives for suspended or expelled students (Michie, 2001; Skiba, Peterson, & Williams, 1997).

By the same token, civil rights groups as well as researchers have noted that students of color, especially African American and Latino youth, are disproportionately affected by the unfair administration of zero-tolerance polices (Advancement Project/Civil Rights Project, 2000; Gordon, Della Piana, & Keleher, 2000; Skiba et al., 1997). Proponents of zero-tolerance policies assert, "If you do the crime, you do the time." In other words, they have argued that the suspension and expulsion of youth of color, especially in urban school districts, is indicative of their deviancy. If this, in fact, were true, then research that demonstrates administrator compliance with zero-tolerance polices would be critical to support this proposition. Alternatively, differential perceptions related to and administration of zero-tolerance policies would support the perspectives that not only are zero-tolerance policies not fully supported by all school administrators, but also that the value of these policies in supporting the developmental pathways of youth needs to be questioned. In other words, some would argue that nonpunitive expulsions or suspensions do nothing to provide a developmental or educational foundation to promote interpersonal development and competency. By the same token, not all acts of "behavioral disruption" warrant punitive discipline. In other words, the opportunity to teach community, moral, and ethical values is lost by simply "removing the problem" rather than building on the teachable moment.

There are additional unintended consequences to this policy that can be attributed to issues of interpretation and implementation. That is, some districts have interpreted the law from a lens that reflects their particular community and cultural perspective, whereas others have complied strictly with the law, perhaps also reflecting the culture of their community, however, in a very different way (Dunbar & Villarruel, 2002). For example, in our earlier study of a Midwest rural community in which hunting is a critical fabric embedded in its culture, we discovered that a student possessing a weapon (provided it is concealed in one's automobile) is not subject to search and prosecution provided the student is not in the parking lot showing it to other students (Dunbar & Villarruel, 2002). That is, it is "out of sight out of mind." Although the administrator may suspect that students have weapons in preparation for hunting after school, it is not viewed as a realistic threat to the safety of students or a violation of Michigan's zero-tolerance policies. The assumption held is one that honors the hunting culture of the community. One administrator asserted, "My father hunted with me and I hunt with my son" (Dunbar & Villarruel, 2002). In this instance, zero tolerance is viewed as an encroachment on the quintessential fabric of the community's cultural identity.

Another example of how this policy is arbitrarily imposed surfaced during our presentation to the Michigan School Board Association on student expulsions (Dunbar & Villarruel, 2002). A rural school administrator disclosed that he told a student (whom he knew had a rifle in his car, presumably to go hunting after school) to turn his car around and return his gun home. However, another case involved an urban school student, whose electronic beeper went off in school, triggering a search of his vehicle, where a shotgun was discovered. In the latter incident, the student was charged with gun possession and now faces a 20-year prison sentence.

The Context of the Problem

The implementation of zero-tolerance policies has generated growing public concern from parents, school administrators, law enforcement agencies, and civil liberty groups over a law that has condemned children to a year or more without a free public education. When initially developed and implemented, there may have been a general perception that free public education is a guaranteed right. Yet, as noted in the United Nations Convention on the Rights of the Child, public education in the United States is not a constitutional right (Walker, Brooks, & Wrightsman, 1999). Thus federal or state statutes do not mandate schools to provide educational alternatives for children who have been suspended or expelled for egregious behavioral acts.[1] Parents who are concerned with minimizing the academic impact of suspension or expulsion are forced to identify affordable and accessible educational alternatives for their children (e.g., home schooling, private schools, or transporting or moving their child to a different school district willing to admit these students).

However, for many students, zero-tolerance laws have exceeded their intended purpose and, in short, have violated the civil rights of youth (Fine & Smith, 2001; Jackson, 2001). In particular, recent studies indicate that the civil rights of African American and Latino children have been disproportionately violated (Ayers et al., 2001; Johnson, Boyden, & Pittz, 2001). For example, the Chicago Public Schools experienced a dramatic increase in the number of expulsions to 737 in 1998–1999 from 14 in 1992–1993. African American students represented 73% of those expelled but only 53% of student enrollment. Latino students represent 20% of those expelled. The number of expulsions increased the following year to 1,500 (Johnson et al., 2001).

This disturbing trend, unfortunately, only reinforces the public perception that African American and Latino youth are somehow more prone to engaging in criminal and juvenile acts. Due to this misconception, questions are raised as to whether zero-tolerance policies are applied differentially across and within school districts. Opponents of zero-tolerance policies assert that the policies are differentially applied and more often affect African American and Latino youth.

Regardless of one's perspective, the implementation of zero-tolerance policies in Michigan—and other states throughout the nation—raises serious questions. Is there a perception of African American and Latino students that predisposes them to stricter adherence to zero-tolerance policies? Has a perceived urban adolescent street culture crossed the school boundaries, thus requiring Draconian and paramilitary tactics to ensure a safe school environment? Is there a socially constructed image of African American and Latino students that has manifested itself into an institutional context of schools that governs disciplinary actions? Are zero-tolerance policies interpreted, implemented, and, hence, enforced more strictly in urban districts, resulting in a greater number of expulsions and suspensions? These questions were explored through a policy analysis framework that sought to understand urban principals' perceptions and implementation of zero tolerance.

---

[1] In Michigan, youth who are expelled for egregious acts, such as weapons, assaults, and sexual acts, are prohibited from enrolling in any public school within Michigan.

Conceptual Lens

In this article, we used a policy analysis framework to analyze responses from principals on the impact of zero-tolerance policy on their administrative duties. We used a variation of a policy analysis framework introduced by Downey (1988) from his work titled *Policy Analysis in Education*. Downey's work provided strategies of analysis that allowed us to acquire information to examine the impact of zero-tolerance policies on the principals' administrative responsibilities. His work introduced various stages that involved a policy analysis process that includes comprehension, initiation, and implementation. Our use of comprehension is concerned with the specific guidelines and procedures involved with the policy. The initiation stage is concerned with determining whether a policy is needed. It entails scanning the environment to assess needs, look for trends, and forecast future trends. Interpretation explores how the policy is understood. That is, what does the policy mean, and what are the parameters that dictate its subsequent implementation? Implementation involves installation of the policy according to the legislative intent. It is the responsibility of the school leader to ensure that the policy is understood and administered equally across the board. These stages are explored further in the discussion of the findings (Figure 1).

Stage 1: Comprehension is concerned with the general knowledge of the zero-tolerance policy held by school leaders
- Understanding of zero-tolerance policies

Stage 2: Initiation seeks to determine the need for the zero-tolerance policy.
- Need for zero-tolerance policies
- Policies or procedures existed before zero-tolerance policies
- Application of zero-tolerance policies
- Revisiting and modifying zero-tolerance policies

Stage 3: Interpretation examines how the policy is understood. That is, what does the policy mean, and what are the parameters that dictate its subsequent implementation?
- Perceptions of school leaders
- Social construction of "bad youth"
- Snap suspensions

Stage 4: Implementation involves installation of the policy according to the legislative intent. It is the responsibility of the school leader to ensure that the policy is understood and administered equally across the board.
- Implementation of Michigan's zero-tolerance policies?
- Noncompliance among principals
- Knowledge of amended policy

Figure 1. Conceptual lens for analysis of urban leaders' responses.

Methodology

The District

The community in which the study was conducted is described as urban and predominantly African American. Based on the 2000 census, this district has a total population of just under 124,753 residents, approximately 53.2% of whom were reported to be Black or African American and 41.4% non-Hispanic White Americans. There are approximately 37,924 children under the age of 18, of which 61% live with a single parent, grandparent, other relative, or nonrelative. Based on data provided by the school district, there are approximately 22,000 students who attend 42 traditional public schools and 5 other schools, including an alternative, such as an Edison school, Adult Learning, Skill Center, and School of Choice. The student racial composition comprises 75% African American, 17.1% non-Hispanic White, 2.4% Hispanic, and approximately 5% divided between Asian and Native American students.

The school district is nestled in an urban community visibly eroding as a result of abandonment caused by the flight of its economic anchor, General Motors. The district includes 4 high schools, 4 middle schools, and 34 elementary schools. The district was selected because educators and members of the community raised concerns about the impact zero-tolerance policy had on their students. The district has used metal detectors and security guards in the high schools and middle schools. Surveillance cameras scan the elementary school grounds, and all staff wear picture identification badges. The main entrances to many of the schools are no longer used. Instead, the entrance closest to the parking area is used. Most of the schools that were visited had some staff member responsible for school security. The Central Office employs a Safety Officer and a Director of Pupil Personnel charged with handling all safety and expulsion issues. Posters displayed throughout most of the school buildings make it difficult to forget that school safety is a high priority.

Probing further, we discovered that these security measures predate Michigan's zero-tolerance policy. In some instances, the security measures had been in place since 1993. In addition, this district has a code of conduct handbook for students that extensively outlines what constitutes inappropriate behavior and the resultant consequences for violating the conduct code. Many references were made to this handbook during the course of our interviews. We believe it is safe to conclude that embedded within the culture of this school district is a critical component involving school safety. Therefore, we asked school principals to explain their understanding of zero-tolerance policy and their implementation of the policy.

The Participants

The researchers sent letters to all principals in the district. Thirty-six out of the 45 principals were from a Midwest urban school district who agreed to participate in the study. Twenty-two were African American respondents and were administrators in 17 elementary, 3 middle, and 2 high schools. Fourteen principals were European American, of whom 11 were from elementary schools, 1 was from a middle school, and 2 were from high schools. Twenty of the principals were men, and 16 were women.

Data Collection

To explore the impact of zero-tolerance policy on the duties of urban school leaders, we generated a series of protocol questions. These were used in face-to-face interviews with 36 out of the 42 school principals working in an urban school district. Administrators who agreed to participate in this investigation participated in a 2-hr structured interview in their environment of choice. The first set of questions allowed principals to reflect on what they knew about the intent of Michigan's zero-tolerance legislation. The researchers wanted to learn how much these urban principals knew about zero-tolerance policies and whether there was consistency across their responses. We followed this query with a question that sought to understand whether school administrators were aware that Michigan's policy had been amended and to what extent the amendment changes affected their understanding and implementation of the policy. The researchers developed additional questions that explored the impact of zero tolerance on teachers, students, and staff in general and what impact the ability to snap suspend students had on teachers. We ended the interviews by asking these principals if they were able to talk with policymakers about their perceptions of the zero-tolerance policy.

Data Analysis

The data were analyzed utilizing a cross-case analysis. As patterns from the data emerged, we simultaneously compared and contrasted them to data already collected. The data were organized into a matrix based on the conceptual framework. A cross-case narrative was written based on the themes that emerged (Huberman & Miles, 1994; see Figure 1). We used

Downey's (1988) stages of policy analysis as a way to understand how these schools' leaders interpreted and implemented the zero-tolerance policy.

As a way to ground our forthcoming discussion of the findings, it is important to present information related to the number of zero-tolerance expulsions that had been documented within this school district during the prior academic year. During the 2000–2001 year, 25 students were expelled from the school district. Of those expelled, 13 were African American females, 10 were African American males, and 2 were male and non-Hispanic white. Ninety-two percent of the students expelled were African American. Analysis of Michigan's zero-tolerance policy also revealed that possession of a knife with a blade longer than 3 in. was the most-often-cited reason for expulsion and accounted for 56% of the documented expulsions. There were three cases of threatening bodily harm, two cases of physical assault on students, one of which included possession of a razor, three gun possessions, one arson, one drug possession, and one bomb threat. The grade level from which students were expelled started at Grade 6 and went through Grade 11. Most of them occurred either in the 9th grade (40%) or in Grades 6 through 8, which made up another 40%. The 10th and 11th grades rounded out the other 20%. Review of these data may indicate the complexity of how schools' leaders may have perceived Michigan's policy on zero tolerance.

Findings

We used Downey's (1988) stages of policy analysis as a lens through which the researchers could understand (a) urban school principals' knowledge regarding zero-tolerance policies and their perceived need for such a policy and (b) their subsequent interpretation and implementation of this policy. Use of Downey's stages of policy analysis provided us with the opportunity to assess these urban school leaders' responses to zero tolerance and their responsibility in implementing the legislated policy.

Another aspect of this study was to examine how this policy influenced the principals' leadership decisions. Most of the existing literature on leadership focuses on organizational theory, decision making, and top-down or bottom-up theories of administration. However, much less research is devoted to understanding the responsibility of leaders to interpret and subsequently implement legislated policy. Findings from this study detailed urban administrators' responses on the impact of zero-tolerance policy on their administrative responsibilities and how it subsequently affected urban students, the majority of whom were African American in this district. This discussion is organized around four stages of Downey's (1988) policy analysis. These stages include comprehension, initiation, interpretation, and implementation (see Figure 1).

Comprehension

Downey's (1988) first stage, comprehension, is concerned with how well school administrators understand (in this case) zero-tolerance policies. Specific knowledge of the intent of the policy will determine how it is interpreted and subsequently implemented. That is, the more informed principals are about the policy, the more apt they are to render an appropriate response to students' behavior. We therefore asked principals to describe their understanding of the zero-tolerance policy.

Understanding of zero-tolerance policies. Perceptions of perspectives of zero-tolerance policies varied among principals. They ranged from a comprehensive understanding to a very narrow view. One high school principal responded,

> From what I understand zero tolerance will not allow students to bring guns and bring violence to the schools. If a student brings a weapon to school, that there will be specific punishment that will come towards that child (de)pending on the severity of what the child had done or what the child had brought.

Another principal's response best represented the general understanding of zero tolerance held by the majority of respondents, stating,

> My understanding is any youngster that brings a weapon to school whether it be a knife, gun or any kind of a weapon that could cause bodily harm is suspended for the duration of the semester or the year or whatever. I don't know exactly what the terms are, but that's my understanding of the zero-tolerance policy.

It appears that despite national attention surrounding zero-tolerance policies, the depth at which the policies were understood varied from one principal to the next. Most responses were prefaced with "what I understand," which suggested that there was no single definitive understanding or clear knowledge of the policy's content. Their interpretation of the policy depended on the school, the grade level, and their understanding. These principals' understanding may explain in part why the punishments they doled out in response to the policy varied from building to building, district to district, city to city, and state to state.

For some administrators, there was confusion about what constituted a punishable offense, as reflected by questions such as, "What if a toy gun is found in a student's backpack?" or "What should be done to a student who tells another student 'I'm gonna kill you' while they're playing?" One principal responded, "I'm going to use common sense," whereas another responded, "I don't allow anything to go by. And if necessary I suspend when there's a weapon or a verbal assault or something like that." What was clear was that some principals considered zero-tolerance policy in every act of behavior by children. It didn't seem to matter whether it posed a real danger to the school or not. Administrators were unclear in their interpretations, which resulted in zero-tolerance policies taking on a life of their own. These principals varied on their interpretation; therefore, was the purpose of the policy to make schools safer or to punish perpetrators?

Initiation

The initiation stage is concerned with determining whether a zero-tolerance policy is needed (Downey, 1988). These principals were asked whether there was a need for zero-tolerance policies. Garnering knowledge of whether principals perceived the zero-tolerance policy as essential assisted the researchers in understanding these principals' willingness to grapple with its intricacies. Thus, understanding the policy assisted the principals in making informed decisions. If the policy were not viewed as necessary, did it affect how it was interpreted and implemented? We asked the principals to offer their perspectives on the necessity of this policy to address inappropriate student behavior (see Figure 1).

Need for zero-tolerance policies. The initiation stage addressed the question of whether or not there was a real policy need and whether or not the policy-making process should have been activated (Downey, 1988). The initiation stage involved an "environmental scanning" process that involved three basic features. The first feature suggested that an assessment of needs and demands occurred to determine how they may be shifting. The second required an assessment of the slippage (i.e., the degree to which subtle shifts in the policy have to be made by administration as opposed to strict application to the policy) that may have occurred between existing policies and the programs they had spawned for the delivery of service. The third feature required an accounting of ongoing trends and anticipation of the future and assessing the future that may be overtaking existing policies, thus rendering them obsolete (Downey, 1988). Thus, we examined the principals' responses to the policy using this lens.

Policies or procedures existed before zero-tolerance policies. One theme raised during many of the interviews was the handbook of student conduct or code for student conduct. The handbook outlined in detail the rules, regulations, and responsibilities of students, parents, and staff necessary for maintaining an educational environment conducive for maximum learning. According to the principals, the handbook was updated every year, and students were provided with a copy. It was "the bible" for governing student behavior. Some principals indicated that in the past, copies had been sent home to family members to familiarize them with school rules. Therefore, did this district need a zero-tolerance policy? One principal responded,

> The district prepares a student code of conduct and every student gets a copy. I have been informed that there is a new copy coming, and they keep it updated quite often. We make sure every student has a copy. Every school is required and encouraged to have an assembly where we discuss these rules with the kids so students will know it. We schedule an assembly program the first week of school. These activities were in place before zero tolerance.

Still another responded,

> We had parent meetings and talked about different policies. The code of student conduct is sent home with students. When parents come in for parent conferences, or one on one conference, we discuss the code of student conduct and lay it out for them as far as what the repercussions are for inappropriate behavior.

One might think that with such an emphasis placed on the rules, there would not be room for variance of interpretation of the policy. Therefore, these principals had a structure in place for examining student conduct, yet they grappled with their administrative decisions.

Application of zero-tolerance policies. Many principals indicated that this district had a policy in place that would address a situation in which a student brought a weapon to school. "We already know what to do if a student brings a weapon to school." However, there were differences in the way principals dealt with a child who brought a toy gun to school. One principal simply collected it and called the parent to explain the policy. This was done to make the parents aware that a second offense of the policy would lead to a suspension. In another situation, a parent had to come to school to retrieve the toy, and in still another instance the child was suspended for a few days. The multiple interpretations indicated that variance of the zero-tolerance policy did occur. Instead of a policy that governed behavior uniformly, these principals arbitrarily implemented the policy. Thus, this resulted in a departure from the policies' original intent.

Revisiting and modifying zero-tolerance policies. Further examination of ongoing trends made clear that the overwhelming increase in the number of expulsions was not anticipated. As a result of public outcry, policymakers have been called on to reassess the increased number of student expulsions. The debate about the policy continued without any sense of resolution. Zero-tolerance policies in some form or fashion existed in the majority of school districts across the country.

Interpretation

Interpretation, the third stage of Downey's (1988) policy analysis, involves how the policy is understood. That is, what does the policy mean, and what are the parameters that dictate its subsequent implementation? Therefore, (a) is the interpretation of the policy critical to its implementation? (b) Is the policy interpreted the same across all principals or is it arbitrarily understood resulting in a variety of ways in which similar violations are addressed? and (c) Does the interpretation of this policy provide school leaders with a guide to address inappropriate student behavior consistently?

Perceptions of school leaders. How a principal interpreted this policy determined how it was implemented. The question became, from what lens do these principals interpret zero-tolerance policy? W. I. Thomas postulated a theorem that suggests "If men define situations as real they are real in their consequences" (Thomas as quoted in Collins, 1988). This theorem has far-reaching implications with regard to how principals viewed the school community and the students who attended these schools. If security guards, metal detectors, and surveillance equipment met students as they entered their school building, did the presence of all of this enhance the potential for violence? That is, was this the creation of a self-fulfilling prophecy? How the school and community situation is defined in effect determines how students are viewed. Blumer suggested that "human beings act towards things on the basis of the meanings which these things have for them. Everything that people act upon or that has an impact on them must go through the process of subjective meaning" (Blumer as quoted in Collins, 1988). If a school community is thought to be riddled with crime, and the children who live in these communities attend the community school, then the children are constructed as criminals. Consequently, students are treated as such. The treatment is manifested in the social construction of these children.

Social construction of "bad youth." How did the perception and subsequent definition of this situation help to shape the construction of the image of urban students of color? Another issue may be how this social construct influenced these administrators' interpretation of the policy. A study by the Applied Research Center, *Racial Profiling and Punishment in U.S. Public Schools* (Johnson et al., 2001), found that schools with 50% or more students of color were more likely to use strict security measures than schools that predominantly served White students. This perception suggests that students of color are perceived as having greater propensity to be involved in acts of violence. This social construct implies that students in urban schools need constant surveillance and cannot be trusted. This depiction aptly fits a criminal. The apparatus in place models the equipment used in prisons. If students are regarded as potential criminals that only await their next crime and the design and staffing of schools place a strong emphasis on catching and punishing perpetrators through equipment, extra security, and policy, then the consequence for these children may end up relegating them to lower educational opportunities. What must be the mind-set of the leadership in these school communities? Does the portrayal of these children as criminals teach administrators to fear students of color? Did this policy and its implementation perpetuate a school culture that portrayed these children as potential scholars or as constructed predators and superpredators? An analysis of these principals' interpretive practices could imply that they socially constructed their students of color as "bad youth."

Snap suspensions. As part of Michigan's zero-tolerance policy, "snap suspensions" were established. These suspensions allowed teachers to suspend a student from their class for up to 1 full school day based on their interpretations of student behavior. Although paperwork is involved, snap suspensions do not require an internal review or a disciplinary review of the perceived behavior situation. For this study, administrators were asked, "To what extent are snap suspensions utilized in your schools?" These principals' responses varied according to grade level, school building, and administrator. Many elementary school principals reported that snap suspensions were limited in their schools. This may have occurred because students were with the same teacher all day and not for a single class period. One principal responded,

> The staff here doesn't feel the need to use it. We work very cooperatively in terms of student discipline. If a youngster and a teacher are having a problem, nine times out of ten we have already discussed the concerns and that youngster is sent to me so that I can deal with him or her. So I'm reasonably sure that we've had only two this year. However, when the law officially came about, there was a rash of snap suspensions.

Still another response stated,

> When I first came here in November, it seemed like every day we were having a suspension. On any given day, a teacher could have at least half of her students leave that day and it has happened. I mean, I haven't been able to see the difference in this kind of suspension and the regular suspension, because it's for the same violation except it's only for a day. The principal still can override the teachers and sometimes its necessary. Sometimes you have teachers (I hate to say it), who are short wired and they exercise zero tolerance for anything. There are some teachers who will come and say that a student rolled his eyes at me and I want him to have a day off.

Both administrators and teachers have the tools to enforce compliance to zero-tolerance rules. That is, administrators had the power to recommend yearlong suspensions, whereas teachers have had the capacity to snap suspend students from their classes for a day. It became apparent that overzealous teachers made snap suspensions even if students "rolled their eyes" allegedly at teachers. Based on information collected, teachers' and administrators' interpretations of these policies indicated students of color were in need of advocates to protect them.

Implementation

Downey's (1988) fourth and final stage, implementation, involves the installation of the policy according to the legislative intent. It is the responsibility of the school leader to ensure that the policy is understood and administered equally across the board. We therefore sought to understand whether school leaders implemented the policy with consistency. That is, were comparable student infractions treated with the same disciplinary actions across schools?

Implementation of Michigan's zero-tolerance policies. The implementation process (in this instance) was examined by an assessment of how principals complied with the zero-tolerance policy. How these leaders interpreted this policy was based on their beliefs about the community and how they have subsequently made it a part of their school culture. In response to a query about the impact of zero tolerance on their administrative duties, principals' responses again ranged from little or no impact to an enormous impact on their duties. For example, one elementary school principal responded,

> If there is any inkling of anyone even having any type of weapon or anything of that nature in school, they immediately are reported to me. Now it becomes a problem that occurs because of this policy. There have been times when a student was in possession of things that were questionable and rather than having staff deal with that, I would much rather have them have to turn those things over to me and let me make that determination. I have to take each situation seriously. So that's affected me to the point where I can't take any chances of that kid saying that "I was just playing" or something like that. It takes a great deal of time because there's a lot of investigative work that has to go on and . . . For example, yesterday, we spent two hours dealing with an issue and you could spend all day sometimes trying to, work around the issue and figure out the truth and getting all the people involved, parent wise, into the building. So it takes a great deal of time.

Most of the principals indicated that they took zero-tolerance policies very seriously. They did not recognize these policies as an encroachment on the culture of their school community. Rather, in some instances, these state regulations were perceived as a tool that took away the "gray area," as was made evident from one principal's comment.

> I think it cleans up that area of how you deal with certain issues and it makes it black and white. When something happens, you know what the consequence will be for that particular action. So it takes that gray area out of it and makes things a lot easier. I welcome the zero tolerance policy. And I think it sort of builds in a safety defense for us because,

you know, we are very vulnerable. Our doors are open. When someone walks in, we don't know what will take place. We just don't know.

For this principal, the outside elements (i.e., the community) placed the school in a vulnerable position, a position that required protection. The administrator was concerned that the additional security and surveillance made students of color not trust them. Perhaps, the message to these children, locked in buildings with a single entrance, cameras that survey both inside and outside the building, additional security, and metal detectors, was to be afraid or to at least be leery of people with whom they live; that is, the good and perhaps not so good people. How were students in urban schools able to make the distinction?

However, in some cases, administrators indicated that the policy served as a guide to aid them in making such distinctions between the "good and the not so good" students. It helped them make decisions about discipline concerns that seemed questionable. Some principals believed that the law took the responsibility of expulsion and suspension out of their hands because of its strict guidelines and what constituted grounds for expulsion. The policy protected these students from external repercussions.

Noncompliance among principals. Coombs (1980) stated, "One may refuse to comply with a policy because of misgivings about the policy itself." He suggested that there exist two kinds of policy-based noncompliance. In the first instance, there are "goal-based noncompliance values." He suggested that issues of this nature are more difficult to change in the short term because values are at stake, for instance, the value held by some principals that children belong in school and should not be expelled for nonthreatening behavior. The second instance involves belief-based noncompliance, or "beliefs about the probable effects of the prescribed behavior." In this instance, the reference was to principals who believed that if a student were expelled, there should be an alternative to address the educational needs of these students. This represented that to expel a student without a viable alternative was objectionable to principals who believed that all children should be provided an opportunity to get a quality education.

Some principals recognized that there were abuses of the policy by some members of their faculty. One principal indicated that because she did not support teachers' snap suspending students (sometimes on a whim), the use of the snap suspension to simply get rid of a student began to wane. In this instance, the principal became an advocate for students by not complying with a policy that supported teacher snap suspensions as the sole means to address a behavior concern. We suspected that there were more instances of noncompliance, so we thought it was important to examine reasons for this resistance.

We believed there were more principals who fell into the preceding categories than the interviews revealed. For these principals, strict adherence to this policy constituted a violation of the rights of children to an education and their own sense that children did belong in school. One principal, when asked about sending a child home for behavior issues, responded,

> When I think about the children here, half of them don't have anywhere to go if we send them home. Going home often means they will be by themselves. I took a child home the other day and I asked what punishment will this child get and the grandmother said, "Nothing. She'll look at TV all day cuz her momma's not here." I said, put your coat on we're going back to school. I gave her an in-school suspension. I had her sit in the hallway with a lesson. So she'll come back all ready to do it again. She's learned nothing from this experience. If taking them home would help, I would do it. But it's not going to help.

Unfortunately, the principals' perception that the students did not learn much from such experiences may be a misnomer. Students soon understood that there was no connection between the school culture and the home environment. The students also realized there was limited dialogue between the principal and their caretakers. The students recognized that the principal did not think they were getting support from their families. There was a perception that the caretakers were not responsible and perhaps lacked interest in their children's education, based on these principals' reactions. The students walked away with the impression that there was something wrong with either their parents or principals. In any case, the students were the ultimate losers. Finally, the students learned that there were minimal consequences for their perceived inappropriate behavior. This was probably one of the most important lessons students learned all week. Principals wanted to do what they thought was in the best interest of the students. Some principals were left with a sense of hopelessness resulting in their stricter enforcement of zero-tolerance policy.

Knowledge of amended policy. Michigan's zero-tolerance policy legislation was revisited in 1996, 1 year after its installation, because school board hearings had begun to be overwhelmed with expulsion hearings. Initially the policy mandated that all alleged violations of the policy be brought before the school board for a hearing. As a result of the increased numbers, the policy was amended to give administrators more discretion to take into account individual circumstances. When asked about their knowledge of the amended policy, the overwhelming majority of principals were not aware that the policy was amended. One principal responded,

> Well, when you said that, I kind of laughed. Like the revised policy, there is one? All I know is basically we get memos from our office of school safety. You read those, you put them away and you go back to business and I could not tell you that I remembered reading that to know exactly what it was. And then sometimes they give you the actual bill, which—oh, man, is that ever rough to try to read and figure out what they want.

Still another responded,

> I'm not really that sure about it. I just know that there were some changes that were made and I think it was made that we would be more severe and act in a different manner. We were a little more lenient before and then we had to really be strict about it after that.

This principal believed that the change must have meant principals needed to be harsher when dispensing punishment. Is this a peculiar way of thinking about the safety of children? Is there a distinction made between the victims and the criminals, or are they perhaps seen as one and the same?

There were other principals who did not feel as compelled to follow zero tolerance to the letter of the law. Their interpretation and implementation of the policy allowed them to give children second chances. They were clear that if a student brought a gun or a knife to school, they were expelled. However a shoving match or an elementary school student who brought a plastic toy gun to school would not be automatically result in suspension. One principal responded,

> I give children the benefit of the doubt, thinking, you know you messed up, you had a bad day or whatever, just don't do it again or you know what's going to happen. The majority of the time that works out, and you know, I've been very successful.

Another principal stated,

> I have not had an instance where a student brought a weapon to school. The weapons that I've confiscated have all been plastic. In my

position as an elementary principal many children, unfortunately, are given a plastic gun as a gift. I'm not about to put up signs in the building that says "no weapons" because I think a whole lot of that kind of environmental reading is just kind of insight to say, "Let me see, how does this work?" So I don't do that. I make the assumption that it's not going to happen and when and if it happens, I'll deal with it. But, I just don't constantly parade talk about it because all it does is keep it on the mind. We have an assembly in the beginning of the year, I go over the district policy and that's the end of it.

Conclusions and Reflections

In the study on which this article is based, we specifically sought to understand how school leaders interpreted and implemented the zero-tolerance policy and how their administrative actions subsequently affected students of color. The most disturbing conclusion revealed by these findings was that there were as many interpretations of the policy as there were respondents (school leaders). Given the grave consequences for students of color, principals' interpretations resulted in the disparate implementation of this policy. There is need to reexamine the leaders' interpretation of this policy and the intended and unintended consequences for students of color. Clearly, the intended objective of the policy was to ensure the safety of students and staff in our schools; however, its inequitable implementation raised concerns about its judiciousness for all students.

Our interviews and observations revealed varied perceptions of the policy among the principals, despite the notion that policy was designed to guide compliance in a prescribed definitive way. However, we have discovered the difficulty in applying this policy equitably across all circumstances. Part of the reason can be explained by the multiple interpretations among the principals. Other reasons may be the way in which the policy was implemented. Factors that influence these principals' implementation included the age and grade of a student, whether a student was a first-time offender, whether the offense truly posed a threat to school safety, or whether there was a parent at home to provide support for the principal who made a discipline decision. Finally, in some instances, there was clearly a lack of awareness by school administrators about the policy and its subsequent amendment. There were vague comments that alluded to parts of the policy; however, from these amendments a substantive comprehensive understanding was not conveyed.

Many principals exercised compassion and common sense when it came to dispensing punishment. One principal indicated that she placed her emphasis on character building among her students. She explained that many of her children don't get this kind of nurturing at home. Is it their fault? Although a rhetorical question, it shed light on the perception that the teacher has about the parents in her school community. Is there a sense by many principals in urban schools that they are in a fight by themselves to educate their students? We wonder how many of these principals would prefer to say that parents are their best tool rather than zero-tolerance policy. Is support given to zero-tolerance policy as a tool in lieu of a preferred parent and hence community support?

We did not ask principals if they thought the community was served by their school. Although some principals described their neighborhoods as "communities with crack houses," they still were unsure what their role was in responding to the community's needs. These principals' responses also indicated that some families were economically disadvantaged. However, these principals did not assume that poor equated students of color with being viewed as dangerous or criminal in nature. After visiting these schools and interviewing principals, it was clear what stood out was the institutional response to what we have deemed the social construction of students of color.

The cameras, added security, the need for name badges worn by school personnel, the metal detectors, and the zero-tolerance policy are all institutional responses that implicitly say, "Students should be watched, searched, and where financially possible security should beefed up." Is there a perception of African American and Latino students that predisposes them to stricter adherence to zero-tolerance policy? Has a perceived urban adolescent street culture crossed the school boundaries, thus requiring paramilitary tactics to ensure a safe school environment? Is there a socially constructed image of African American and Latino students that is manifested in an institutional context of schools that govern disciplinary actions? Unfortunately, based on these principals' responses, the answer is yes.

Clearly, Michigan's zero-tolerance policies are a necessary evil. The public desires safe schools that promote safe learning environments. But as noted in these findings, the current policies alone do not fully achieve this outcome. Administrators interviewed for this study questioned whether these policies were "in the best interest of school-aged youth." In short, the administration and implementation of Michigan's zero-tolerance abdicate their individual and school-level responsibility to provide educational opportunities for students of color. These principals' focus on removing students of color was not viewed as a punitive approach for behavioral disruptions or troubled behaviors.

Concurrently, the implementation of zero-tolerance policies has negatively affected the opportunities for administrators and teachers to develop mentoring and positive relationships with their students. Instead of exercising and demonstrating caring relationships and environments, schools are becoming hostile environments where positive behaviors are ignored and the "surveillance" of bad behavior is recognized. Cameras, bars on windows, and locked doors may actually minimize safe and quality learning environments rather than foster them.

Finally, as a community of scholars, we must ask whether zero-tolerance policies are influencing our view of youth and whether youth themselves perceive that adults have developed a new worldview of them. Have our nation's policy leaders developed a social construction of students of color that suggests that their purposeful or unintended engagement in what are not socially accepted behaviors will result in a lifetime of egregious and criminal acts? Have teachers developed a view that only some children can learn? Although an evaluation of zero-tolerance policies is undoubtedly needed, the scholarly community must also expand our understanding of the impact that these policies have on the educational and developmental pathways of youth.

References

Advancement Project/Civil Rights Project. (2000). *Opportunities suspended: The devastating consequences of zero tolerance and school discipline.* Washington, DC: Author. Retrieved from http://www.law.harvard.edu/groups/civilrights

Ayers, W., Dohrn, B., & Ayers, R. (2001). *Zero tolerance: Resisting the drive for punishment in schools.* New York: Free Press.

Collins, R. (1988). *Theoretical sociology.* San Diego, CA: Harcourt Brace.

Coombs, F. (1980). The bases of noncompliance with a policy. *Policy Studies Journal, 8,* 885–900.

Dohrn, B. (2001). "Look out kid/it's something you did": Zero tolerance for children. In W. Ayers, B. Dohrn, & R. Ayers (Eds.), *Zero tolerance: Resisting the drive for punishment in schools* (pp. 89–113). New York: Free Press.

Downey, L. W. (1988). *Policy analysis in education.* Calgary, Alberta: Detselig Enterprises Limited.

Dunbar, C., & Villarruel, F. A. (2002, April). *School leaders and perceptions of zero tolerance policy in Michigan.* Paper presented at the meeting of the Michigan Association of School Boards, Lansing, MI.

Fine, M., & Smith, K. (2001). Zero tolerance: Reflections on a failed policy that won't die. In W. Ayers, B. Dohrn, & R. Ayers (Eds.), *Zero tolerance: Resisting the drive for punishment in schools* (pp. 256–264). New York: Free Press.

Gordon, R., Della Piana, L., & Keleher, T. (2000). *Facing the consequences: An examination of racial discrimination in U.S. public schools.* Oakland, CA: Applied Research Center.

Huberman, A., & Miles, M. (1994). Data management and analysis methods. In N. Denzin & Y. Lincoln (Eds.), *Handbook of qualitative research* (pp. 428–441). Thousand Oaks, CA: Sage.

Jackson, J. L. (2001). Foreword. In W. Ayers, B. Dohrn, & R. Ayers (Eds.), *Zero tolerance: Resisting the drive for punishment in schools* (pp. vii–ix). New York: Free Press.

Johnson, T., Boyden, J. E., & Pittz, W. (2001). *Racial profiling and punishment in U.S. public schools: How zero tolerance policies and high stakes testing subvert academic excellence and racial equity*. Oakland, CA: Applied Research Center. Retrieved from http://www.arc.org/erase/profiling_nr.html

Ladson-Billings, G. (2001). America still eats her young. In W. Ayers, B. Dohrn, & R. Ayers (Eds.), *Zero tolerance: Resisting the drive for punishment in schools* (pp. 77–85). New York: Free Press.

Michie, G. (2001). Ground zero. In W. Ayers, B. Dohrn, & R. Ayers (Eds.), *Zero tolerance: Resisting the drive for punishment in schools* (pp. 3–14). New York: Free Press.

Michigan Zero Tolerance Policy. (1996). Michigan Complied Laws 380.1311.

Skiba, R. J., Peterson, R. S., & Williams, T. (1997). Office referrals and suspensions: Disciplinary intervention in middle schools. *Education and Treatment of Children, 20,* 295–315.

Walker, N. E., Brooks, C. M., & Wrightsman, L. S. (1999). *Children's rights in the United States: In search of a national policy.* Thousand Oaks, CA: Sage.

For Product Safety Concerns and Information please contact our EU
representative GPSR@taylorandfrancis.com
Taylor & Francis Verlag GmbH, Kaufingerstraße 24, 80331 München, Germany

www.ingramcontent.com/pod-product-compliance
Lightning Source LLC
Chambersburg PA
CBHW061420300426
44114CB00015B/2001